Biography
of a
Soul

✸

MILITZA SEGURA-LANDRAU

Edited by Cleves Book World
www.clevesbooks.com
Special thanks to Militza Fernandez and Ninotchka Fernandez
for their contribution to the correction of the book.

Order this book online at www.trafford.com
or email orders@trafford.com

Most Trafford titles are also available at major online book retailers.

Edited by Cleves Book World
www.clevesbooks.com
Special thanks to Militza Fernandez and Ninotchka Fernandez
for their contribution to the correction of the book.

Printed in the United States of America.

ISBN: 978-1-4251-1715-3 (sc)

Trafford rev. 09/14/2012

www.trafford.com

North America & international
toll-free: 1 888 232 4444 (USA & Canada)
phone: 250 383 6864 ♦ fax: 812 355 4082

Acknowledgements

I WOULD LIKE TO thank the Creating Source of each and all my good inspirations. That Energy that many know with different names but everybody loves with the same intensity: God. His Omnipotence and Omniscience dwelling within my heart removed the veil of my spiritual ignorance.

To my mother, the woman with more determination and strength than I have ever met in my life, for her faith in my artistic talent when nobody else believed in me. To my father, a poet and romantic gentleman, who gave me the inheritance of a muse, and the wonderful treasure of love for reading.

To my siblings who, one way or another, planted their experiences in my life. These were helpful and were also examples in some situations throughout my process of change.

To my daughters, the first human beings who taught me how easy it is to love unconditionally. To my princess Ninotchka, my beloved biological granddaughter, the earthly source that inspires most of my good actions, and the best friend of "My inner child" and who, after God, is responsible for my total healing.

To my husband, a typical Gemini, who would invite me to a restaurant, and then take me to another because he had changed his mind, but who has been extraordinarily stable in giving me support and believing in me during my difficult process.

To the sons in law that my daughters gave me, because they have made me feel like a mother of two loved and respected women and each of them, in their own way, has also demonstrated their love and support to me.

To the two girls who came into my life to satisfy my need to have many descendants, Dara and Carly, the granddaughters of my soul, who have given me one more reason to feel proud. Thank you for the gift of your presence and love.

To the true friends who thank God, I have had. For the beautiful moments that have left traces in my soul with a beautiful fragrance of spring flowers.

And lastly, I would like to thank the people to whom I owe more. They are the ones whom I stretched my hand out to, but they did spit on it; the ones I loved and failed me; the ones who laughed with me, but let me cry alone, the ones who took advantage of me; the ones who killed my illusions. The ones who made fun of my aspirations and to those who never believed in me. Thank you for teaching me the most important step for my change and healing, "Forgiveness". If you had not existed, I would not have been able to learn how to forgive.

Militza Segura-Landrau.

Contents

Preface

IT IS NOT EASY to speak about the person you love without being too flattering, especially when it is about one's mother. However, I believe that nobody knows Militza better than my sister and myself. She was always very open in her expressions and her way of thinking. She did not let any social or religious conventionalism violate her; she used to think in her own way and that was it. She did not care about other people's approval. I believe that in spite of her religious education, deep down she rebelled against the established norms as moral rules, which lacked a solid foundation or unconditional love.

She raised us with a religious education but she tried not to fall in to any fanaticism of abnormal restrictiveness. We did not celebrate birthdays, however, she did allow us to attend our friend's celebrations and she asked us not to sing the happy birthday song. She stayed very calm as she trusted us in a way that if we did not love her and respect her so much, we would have never done what she asked us to do when she was not present. One day she decided that God was in the hearts of everyone and that God did not punish.

Little by little we stopped practicing our religion, but we never refrained from praying, loving God and having a heart full of FAITH, because she, in the middle of her hidden sadness, used to have a happy face for everything. She was always telling jokes and she handled things with a different philosophy than our friends' parents. From the time we were little, she consulted with us and she took our opinions into consideration.

She was a mother to all of our friends, who loved her very much. Some of them would even ask her for advice about their lives at home. Others would not tell us that they wanted a mother like ours. Maybe nobody, not even us in that stage, would realize the amount of conflicts she had.

The truth is that her fight to be the accomplished woman she is today was never really appreciated until we were adults. I cannot say anything negative about my *madrecita*, as I like to call her, because she gave us so much love that there was not any time to think that her internal revolution was hurting her physical health or our tranquility. She remained quiet when she received the medical diagnosis, she shared with her husband only, we only knew about all her suffering when this was finished.

From my childhood I remember our holidays, the beautiful songs that she used to sing for us, her solidarity not only with her family and with her friends and her determination to in being positive when she was really full of traumas and fears. That is why I write this today, to let her know that I love her more than ever and that she is a very special being that I admire.

What she gave us and keeps on giving us is more positive than negative. She is a woman full of unconditional love for all, she never is hurtful to anybody and she treats everyone the same, with the same love. This has sometimes brought us conflict because she has been misunderstood. She is a giving source of energy and happiness. She has concentrated her vision in childhood, with the hope that one day this planet will be inhabited by human beings who know how to give love and with the understanding that their parents give them today. She has not told me, but I know that a percentage of the sale of this book will be donated to a children's hospital in Florida, where she is an anonymous donor. This is my little mother, a very special woman!

Teresa Militza Freeman (Thaimí).

I would like to write about my mother Militza Segura-Landrau, who is one of the most inspirational and strong women that I have ever met.

My mother taught me what self-acceptance and unconditional love was. She is the source of wisdom with a high sense of justice, understanding and patience.

I hope to be able to offer my daughter Ninotchka the same, love, happiness, wisdom and light that she has given me all my life.

I think God for such an incredible mother who has supported me so much. She is a woman who is very special and respectful of individuality. My mother strongly believes in the right of each individual to be who they want to be, even if it is through a difficult path full of mistakes. She thinks that this is an inalienable right that must be respected. She does not judge, criticize or condemn. My mother has always inspired me and she continues to inspire me to give the best of me.

Mami, if when I was little girl I had known what I know today, I would not have made things as difficult for you, I would have understood better how difficult it must have been for you to allow the persons you love the most to learn from their own mistakes. Likewise, I would have realized how fortunate I am to have a mother who is always there for me.

Even if it is too late to go back and change many things, it is not too late to say that I appreciate you very much and I am very thankful for everything you have given us and keep on giving us. It is not too late either to say: "Mami, I love you very much".

Militza Teresa Fernández (Mayte).

"Dear Abuelita Linda"

Congratulations and thank you for being my grandmother and for everything you do for me. Thank you for helping me with my mommy and for the opportunity to celebrate my fifteenth birthday. You are really magnificent. Oh yes, thank you too for being such a great example of happiness, you are my role model.

Ninotchka Ivonne.

To my dear wife:

You can do everything and there is no obstacle you cannot overcome. Everything will turn out well because you put love in to everything you do.

I am not intellectual but that does not prevent me from telling you that I love, admire and respect you very much.

Rubén.

INTRODUCTION

TO LIVE SAYING "I am going to do" is like somebody who complains about a pain but does not look for its remedy. I do not pretend to describe my life story, as it is like many others. Instead, I'd like to review it a little, and in general, to be able to demonstrate that we all can make a positive change in our existence.

Biography of A Soul is born out of a profound desire to show others, that we, ourselves, are our own enemies. That we are our own stumbling block – that we are the cause, but not the effect.

That if we learn to say no to inertia, pain, criticism, impotence and to failure, we will be able to fill our lives with energy; physical, mental and spiritual health; have time to build, power to do, love to give and become an outright success.

Every time we say "I'm going to do" but inactivity defeats us, we start on our way to the negation of everything. Many years went by after I kept gathering poems for a book, which I've been trying to publish for almost all of my life. After making a new year's resolution hundreds of times to publish my poetry book in that year, I came to the conclusion that all of it was nonsense.

Books, like all other things we desire, require planning first, then a decision and finally an execution. Neither a book nor a work gets done by itself in life. Desire must be accompanied by effort, dedication, love and inspiration.

I want to thank a writer for the formation of this book – a writer who found me (metaphorically speaking) sitting on a rock at the edge of a river, trying to fish without casting the rod. I was just taking the fish that other fishermen would generously give me.

He pushed me into the water and I not only learned how to swim, but I also got my own fish. Thank you for helping me find my own compass, thank you because, from now on, not only will I know how to get to a safe harbor, but I will also sail the waters I want to sail.

CHAPTER 1

✳

CAUSE AND EFFECT

"Every action brings a reaction along"

A VICTIM OF EVERYBODY else or just of yourself? Many years ago, I asked myself this. The answer was the true reason of the beginning of my change and the main motivation and inspiration to write this book.

I was deeply entangled with a great number of wrong thoughts and ideas; I had created a monster of mental uselessness, thinking others were lucky, but I was not. All of this was due in part to the excessive attention I received; it was the product of the environment I grew up in. It was the consequence of behaviors around me, erratic enough to confuse me, and of my father's overprotection which I never understood.

I do not remember having big responsibilities. I loved to cook when I was little. I had a kitchen which

"The Three Kings" had brought to me where I pretended to make great meals.

When I was a teenager, I started to experiment with real recipes, hiding and on the quiet with the help of the person in charge of cooking at my house. But I could not. My father told the cook he wanted me out of the kitchen, and that my only obligation was to study. So goodbye to my imaginary recipes. I was never asked, nor allowed, to make my bed or do any kind of work in the house. That was the servants' work. It was easy to avoid this when I was an adult.

In the end, I always felt like a victim of circumstances. With time I grew up without changing my way of thinking. I did not grow up mentally or emotionally in relation to my age. It was easy to blame the overprotection I enjoyed. How comfortable!

How can a human being believe he doesn't have any responsibility when he is already an adult? However, I remember I had, what I considered, an attribute; I've never liked to gossip. It may seem as if this is not related to this book, but you'll find out it is.

I always thought my life was too entangled to worry about others. I'd quickly forget any comment, whether preconceived or not, about me or anyone who was not present to defend himself.

This has always seemed like a hypocritical, vile and cowardly act to me, never mind, of course, that most of the times those comments are full of envy. In other words, as I never saw the mote in another's eye, I never noticed the beam in my own.

In the previous notes you must've noticed that when I was very little I was very spoiled. My mother had had miscarriages before being able to get pregnant with me and give birth. My great grand mother did not die until I was born. She was waiting for my arrival and she wanted to "sweet" me. "Sweet" me is what holding is called in my country just after birth. She was able to do it and she also kept the illusion of having in her arms the descendent of his youngest and spoiled grandson, who was my father.

My father used to anxiously write poems and odes, while he waited and hoped for my arrival. His poem "You, My Son" that he wrote for my mother when I was in my mother's womb, was not only a family success but a social event, It was almost an obligation to recite the poem in the Sunday family gatherings, by my father or my older sister, who was a theatre actress and professional reciter.

My birth was a great event. Advertisements on the society page of the city's main newspapers; fine cards with my photo made in a photograph studio to announce my arrival to the world to relatives and friends.

My older sisters tell me they were in charge of taking the good news to our closest neighbors, proclaiming the arrival of a new family member. I still remember a homemade recording that I listened to when I was a child, where my father, proud of his princess in his arms (or so I was told), asked my mother why I was so spoiled.

Admittedly, my parents and older sisters showed me off as a valuable, beautiful trophy. I have got a nice memory of a Sunday when my oldest sister came home with some friends and she told them, "look, this is my little sister, she's three years old and she already knows how to read." She immediately looked for the color comics in the Sunday newspaper and asked me to read it for them. How proud she felt in front of her friends!

What happened afterwards? I never thought about it during the years I lived swimming in a sea of traumas and trying to be happy in my way, not understanding why I behaved so differently from the rest of my family. I lived a bohemian life, apparently useless. I used to read and write a lot, and the supposed spiritual pain, or my inability to develop a positive personality, helped develop my inspiration to write poems charged with bitterness, as I was.

I visited all kinds of churches looking for a single answer to my so radical difference from the rest of my family. A person once told me that perhaps I was a little crazy, so I went to a psychological session with the hope of finding professional help. The psychologist laughed and said, "bring me the person who told you that; I'm sure that person is the one who needs help."

Years later, after studying psychology, I understood why I was told that. All of what we think about everybody else is our own mind, therefore we are suffering from the same, whether or not we understand or accept it.

My mother had more guts than many men I've ever met; she made a fortune in the real estate business and got married very young, and when the university in the capital started the adults short-term study program towards careers she was already so involved in her own life, she was "not able" to do it, or she thought she couldn't.

I remember the stories my mother's cousin, who was an engineer, used to tell me. He said my mother knew exactly how to make a house plan, and that many of them she made, either he or another engineer would sign the plans to legalize the building permits. And of course, these appeared like plans made by them and these were legally theirs.

Years later, the consulate in our country granted her an engineer's "Honoris Causa" degree for the knowledge she acquired about the profession. How proud I felt that day; how happy she was.

My father, an accountant, was always a well respected executive. We were not millionaires, but I grew up in a comfortable environment, and even a driver from the company my father worked for, was provided to us to take us back and forth to the private school where my youngest sister and I studied.

All of my older sisters were successful entrepreneurs with good lives. My youngest sister with an accounting degree was always a true professional with great achievements both in her professional and personal life. My only brother, an attorney, is also successful and with a very strong personality.

What had happened to distort my own self that had dragged me into the negative to the point that I even attracted people to my life who would envy me and cause me harm? Why, although I had talent for my own profession, could I not have a successful professional life?

How is it possible that yearning for those first years of my childhood, in a home I recalled as almost perfect, did I not even feel I was ready to make my own home? How did I go so wrong in my social and emotional relationships? Did it all have to be that way? Does destiny really exist? If so, why are some born lucky and some not? By any chance, did I ask to come into the world?

If there was a change in my family environment which impressed my mind and changed my path unfavorably, I will not speak about it in this book. Really, I believe I will never do it because it has no relevance. This is not about judging others, but it is about the way in which we all, without exception, can take hold of the reins of our lives. And when I say – we all, I am including even people who haven't had the possibility to study and prepare themselves.

I have met successful entrepreneurs who have succeeded in the United States without speaking English. In my country, I have heard of illiterate farmers who were able to have a small successful business within their business knowledge limitations, and raise their family without even knowing how to write, but they surely learned how to add, divide and subtract, because necessity required them to do so.

It all depends on what success means to you. This is very difficult to depict. There are people who say they are successful because they have it all, even if they have had to sacrifice the time with their family to achieve it. Others believe success is to have all the family going to church in harmony and keep a pretense of a good relationship with God. However, they constantly complain about illness and material lack. I believe success is fighting for happiness. Without a doubt, it is keeping ourselves happy more often than the times we feel unhappy. Happiness is interior peace – abundance of unconditional love in our heart. It is not the things we do or possess, or the people we live with or have a relationship with. These things and these people we enjoy because we are happy; it is the other way around.

Through the years, I have learned all the answers to my questions and many more through profound studies about life, its origin, and why, and what we exist for.

Above all, to gain a great knowledge of myself, to meditate, to search my inner self, and to look for the answers hidden in my subconscious which are nothing but those experiences which made a mark on me in my previous incarnations and have been added to the experiences of my present life.

I learned that every action brings about another reaction, and I began to find for out myself so that I could better understand the Law of Cause and Effect. I began trying to investigate my early childhood which I have nice memories of. What I recalled was big reunions in my home every weekend, my parents dancing, and my little sister dancing while holding on to my mother's skirt.

Everything was so perfect for me – my parents' friends whom I think of as nice people who loved us and who had children the same age. Because of this, my little sister and I had friends to play with, understand, learn from, and teach.

So I started the hard work of getting to know myself: first, by regressing through each of the significant stages of my happy childhood, and from the mistakes made when I was already an adult. Then I started paying honest attention to everything I did and said, feeling and watching my own and others' reactions to my actions, words, and thoughts.

Keeping my distance from people who, with or without intention, made me react and retarded my personal project and personal pro-activitiy and growth. I also watched others and I recognized in their defects and virtues, my own.

How hard it is to believe this, but it is true; nobody comes into our lives without a reason, and, in the same manner, it is not a coincidence that we come into the lives of others. We can be teachers, makers or destroyers of our environment. We will see this later on.

CHAPTER II

✺

THE MOTE IN MY NEIGHBOR'S EYE

REMEMBER WHEN I AFFIRMED that perhaps I always ignored the mote in my neighbor's eye and therefore, I never noticed the beam in my eye? Well, I learned something – that until then it seemed impossible or hopeless. Every person who comes into our lives, no matter from what race, social class, religious or political belief, has such a strong resemblance to us. It is as if we could see ourselves in a mirror which reflects our spirituality, mentality and our personality. It is not easy to accept that a person who we consider demanding, bad mannered or socially awkward is very like us, but the truth is that every human being who comes into our lives teaches us and helps us to change – even those, who life confronts us with, and whom we reject from the deepest part of our being.

We must be honest enough to accept that we are wrong if we leave our ego aside and carefully observe the other person. We'll find two things that are not the same – they end up having the same effect on both our mind and heart. The first thing is that what we detest in that person is what we hate in ourselves. Without recognizing it, we can see to a degree that the person does possess an attribute which seems negative and undesirable to us and which we wouldn't like to have, but we do have it nevertheless.

The second thing that does not necessarily fit with the first, because they are usually separate is envy. Although, it might seem absurd, sometimes we hate in another's lifestyle, character, or personality something we want, but we don't dare to develop this because of social fears, fear of ridicule, of opposing family opinion or hang ups which prevent us from being the real us.

Because that is reality, only when we are who we want to be and we do what comes out of the soul are we happy because we are being real, and not a reflection of our social class – not a depiction of what the family expects from us, nor a continuation of what our parents are or were.

Neither should you be a blind follower of some radical doctrine where they kill the inner part of your spirit just because you must do so, or else, there's an exemplary punishment waiting for you. Nothing that forces us to act a certain way, even though we do it willingly, is, or can, become a motive for happiness.

Freedom or the free will to choose what you want

to do has more value than all the money in the world. If you are happy, you love. If you love, you give. If you give, you receive. And this is how we'll have a perfect existence on a happy planet, where, even though many can't understand it and others can't believe it, we are ONE. We're bound by energy, spiritually and mentally although we coexist in different bodies.

If we understand it, if we accept it, many things in our lives will change. Then we can call ourselves successful.

WISE ADVICE

If you free your emotions, the wind will bring the fruits

WHEN I WAS A child there was a farmer who watched and kept a farmhouse where we lived for a number of years. He said, "never put a bird in a cage." "It would be better taken care of because my father would buy food for it," I answered.

He replied, "you can be sure it is happier living a single day in freedom than many years in a cage." A few years later, I understood that teaching perfectly and I released the canaries, small parrots, and bluebirds that my husband had given me.

By that time, somebody told me they were not ready to be free and would perish -then I recalled and repeated the humble farmer's wise words. What happiness I experienced when I saw them fly towards their true destiny, not the one I had imposed on them.

I was convinced they would survive. The universe makes provision for all. God has created a safe habitat for all, depending on their species. How sure I felt. That day I felt some strange sensations; I wondered how it would be if I also started to fly.

How long would I survive? Would I learn to spread my wings? Would I know how to detect danger while looking for my inner freedom? Yes, I wanted to do it; I just needed decision.

SELF-LEARNING
Be Your Own Master

ONE DAY I WOKE up feeling like changing my life totally. I became determined to concentrate my years of study, learning and searching on just one discipline which would contain all that I had learned in books, talks, seminars and the main way – my own experience.

When I tried to search for the common dimension that filled my spirit and my intellect, I found out it was just one word. This is to say that the answer to my worries, the solution to my "problems" could be reduced to one word that I had heard since childhood, but I never understood it's scope, the positive vibration which manifests in our lives, nor the chain reaction this quality generates. Have you guessed the word? LOVE.

Since the time we were children we have had manifestations of spiritual, physical and material love. Unfortunately, we were never taught at home or church how to really love. It doesn't matter how unconditional our parents' love looks like, we don't perceive the light, only their fears, so the first and only learning experience about love is overprotection. Later, at college and at church, they teach us to be alert against evil.

Therefore, in each situation we face in life, we experience that kind of love, always full of fear, insecurity, and pain. We don't feel capable of succeeding because despite everything, we haven't learned to love. Therefore, we begin a lifestyle which will last all our lives, not knowing what to do with the fire of love inside our hearts. We begin loving our parents with such vehemence that just to think one day they will die, causes a profound pain in us. I remember when I was little I would ask God to let me die first before my parents, because I thought I couldn't endure that pain. Can you identify with this? I know I've heard other people confessing that fear.

Then, the love for our brothers, friends, and toys follows. You notice I always use the word "our" because that is what we've learned. We've got a possessive, binding mentality even from our mother's womb. If you add to this, that your parents make you dependent on their desires, even those parents who believe that a child must be independent, they somehow make them feel like their possession and not a little fellow whom they should help to discover his or her abilities. Then the child can learn to manage his or her freedom in a healthy way, and they can become happy without harming themselves or harming others. As a result, they never feel their lives and interior peace depends upon some binding, whatever this might be. So they don't follow the same pattern with their families when they have one.

MY ATTACHMENTS

"Psychological attachments are spiritual impotence"

THE DAY I DECIDED to quit smoking, and I could do it with no relapse, that day I learned I could overcome anything; I knew it was not an easy task, but I could do it.

I had been smoking for many years and I was a tobacco suicidal-criminal dependent. Yes; because I was not only killing myself slowly, but I was forcing people around me to smoke and get sick, not to mention that I was contaminating the environment.

Everybody knows the consequences, no need to explain them. It is difficult to believe we don't love ourselves, but it is obvious that if you are undermining your life, not only do you not love yourself, but you don't love others. Perhaps somebody may think this is not a big deal, but any smoker who might be reading this book knows how difficult it is to quit smoking, especially when I was already smoking five packs of cigarettes a day. Rather, I believe, after smoking so much, that any person who has a dependence, whatever this might be, must make a big effort to quit. It is not easy.

I have heard too many excuses for not quitting tobacco or for using it again, "I smoke because of anxiety." "I smoke because I like it." "I smoke to control my weight." "I can quit when I want," etc. The truth is that those people lack willpower to do it, or they are really deceiving themselves, because all the above mentioned excuses plus the ones I have not mentioned have other kinds of solutions. For the smoker, tobacco is a kind of god that helps them face their energetic, social or spiritual lack or perhaps all of them together.

When they understand this, they will never dare to give so much importance to one of the greater murderers mankind has. And they will also understand that the love in their hearts is not being used to full capacity; this is why they don't think about harming themselves or harming others. I remember the conclusion I came to when I decided to begin my change.

I learned that my dependence on tobacco was controlled by a stimulus need. I spoiled myself unconsciously looking for those treats I received when I was little, my mother's admiration when I made a picture, my father's pride when he said I was very intelligent and he'd almost drool at the privilege of being my father. Why didn't I grow up emotionally? Why was that need to be spoiled?

Well, I decided to begin pampering myself because I wanted to be spoiled. I gave myself a beautiful gift of life – I quit smoking. That was my first indulgence, and at the same time, my first achievement; I learned I could spoil myself without creating a useless being. I learned that there are healthy and fruit-ful indulgences.

But I still felt anxiety, emptiness, and a feeling that I had lost something, but I did not know what it was. My only hobby was to write poems, embittered, anguished, and sad; products of my mind and spirit that were more confused every day and attacked by the traumas and hang-ups, and I didn't know for sure what produced them.

Friends who would come into my life had the same

lack, so I also wrote and described their lives and experiences in my poetic inspirations. Insecurity overwhelmed me. I couldn't find the link where everything started. I had good friends who helped me a lot spiritually, who told me those sad poems could become songs to life and take beautiful messages to other people.

But it was really until a doctor diagnosed breast cancer in me, that a spark of flight ended forever a life I considered unproductive and empty, although it was not really. I was always a loving and devoted mother.

I was a "mother hen" to the point of enrolling myself in the university when they were studying to "look after them." How absurd – don't you think? You know something, I loved them with the same fear my parents loved me.

Today I love my daughters in a different and profound way. I've never missed an opportunity to demonstrate it to them, and to be there if they need me. I never impose myself, but they know I am there for them because now I have not only two daughters. They gave me a big family, beautiful and united including my sons-in-law and my grandchildren and I love all of them, but the best thing is that I know how to love them.

Imposition, far from helping, is bothersome. I've supported them as much as I've been able and more... even giving up my own beliefs, principles, and strict education. But, going back to the cancer diagnosis, I remember the day when I told my husband he was astonished. He didn't know what to say; he had that fear I've already told you about, because that's what he had also learned. I spoke with a psychologist friend who told me "you have to fight, what would humanity be without you?" I never believed that statement which was just the result of love and respect from a good friend, but how good I felt! It was beautiful to think that humanity needed me.

Later, I learned that, deep inside, he was right; we all need each other without being overly dependent, and at times even if we don't know each other. I was the only one who could take the reins of my life and I began with the changes in my spiritual life, knowing myself as I am, Image and Likeness and therefore, a god creator of my own Universe.

My fight with life to encounter again the princess they made me believe I was in my early childhood was tough. It was not a fairy tale as people understand it; rather it was an intense fight. I still keep fighting to reach and keep my spiritual origin. But I know where I'm going.

When I looked over my life, I found a sad little girl who neglected to grow up right in the moment when her parents got divorced. The body grew up and my inner little girl was left behind in the past. Bingo! I finally have a starting point where to begin work on myself. I have to give joy to the little girl so that when it is manifested in the adult I am now, this manifestation can be a happy one.

I worked on this for years. There's no bitterness. But now and then, some effect from that cause would come to my life. My reaction? I'm still a human being with all the consequences.

But the good news is that I know it now, taking a deep breath I do myself a favor and I relax and the light flows. This is what I had to unearth. If there's no memory, there's no binding. If there's no binding, you are free. If you are free, you are happy. After beginning a period of self-knowledge, of my universal participation in a spiritual and physical life, I also started to work on the famous question which I begin this book with. Am I a victim of others, or a victim of myself? You cannot imagine when I finally understood it, how many times I saw the mote in my neighbor's eye, but not as a criticism now or to judge others, but as a sincere act of comparing them to me so that I can help myself and, finally, have something to offer others, so that in turn, they can help themselves and then help others. It is a necessary chain for human evolution and the universe.

The outbreak of my turning point of progress in myself started to manifest, and I was also sure people who served as a model for me to change, have also gotten better. This is why I wrote this book because I'm sure many others can use me as a mirror and I want to teach them how to make changes in their soul.

Incredible! If I change, people around me also change. In other words, each human behavior has a ripple effect which affects or communicates with people around us. I keep on experimenting; I still use it – this is a change that never ends.

Now I call it "Mutual Help." From that little experiment I learned that if I want to generate positive changes in people around me, the change must start with me.

Another thing I learned was freedom from bindings. It is about this: we create a circumstance in our life we think is good or, at least, we take it as something normal we have to do. But it happens that, as time goes by, we are fed up with this situation and even so, we decide to keep it and we do not dare to take the step and change it. What underlies this? The supposed victim.

Then, complaints against others, friends, family and God (The Universe), comes up. Yes, because in order to fill up the cup, we feel so good that we say to God we accept the burden He's given us. But what is this all about? Is God also in the panorama of traumas and ties? No, you took the burden into your life because of a sense of misplaced responsibility, because you need to show a model image to society; because of a misunderstanding, for what they have to say, because you think you can do everything, because you've got a trauma which you haven't overcome, because you want to test yourself, etc. There can be thousands of answers, but you can be sure none of the answers is that God entrusted you with it.

And if you examine the situation closely, you'll notice there was a lack of love for yourself; therefore, the task you have entrusted yourself with, does not have spiritual value because you are manifesting that you are fed up with the situation. You even use the melodramatic phrase of the afflicted, "this is my cross and I will carry it until the end." What do you think? This phrase does not even sound good anymore. It is so outdated.

It is time to stop blaming God for all we do when the result is bad. When we do something right, we just thank God and keep going, thinking it was really our achievement. We do not sit down to celebrate with God because we really believe He did it through us. And not to mention not everybody says thanks to God, for there are people that don't do it, perhaps they recognize it in their inner self, but they don't say it. I've got friends and relatives who say we shouldn't mention God all the time; it is part of their belief.

I respect that viewpoint but I don't share it. My interaction with the Universe – feeling myself an active part of it has helped me a lot – especially because I do it independently, without thinking that if I fail I will be punished. That is my advantage and it can be yours too.

But going back to our theme to learn how to set ourselves free, or to get to know the truth which will set us free, (not my words of wisdom but I practice them as if they were), the first thing to do is to understand that as soon as we are adults we have the obligation, the capability and the duty to take the reins of our lives and be responsible for what we have done, for what we are doing and for what we will do. We will always have some debts with our "destiny" (Karma, Tikun, Cause and Effect), but the change can make a big difference between what your life is today, and what it was, and believe me, the consequences will also be different and you will be amazed! You will see what your life will become.

Because your future is nothing but today seen as tomorrow, therefore if you want a nice and pleasant one, learn to be happy NOW. I learned that my first marriage was not a failure because that experience left me two daughters whom I love profoundly.

The older one gave me the wonderful present of being a grandmother. I've got a biological granddaughter who in part, has been the vehicle and inspiration that makes me improve a little more every day. I've got two granddaughters from the husband of my youngest daughters that make up my trio of little women of different ages. From them I learn again that each stage is beautiful and productive. All three are honor students, and I? I feel proud when I say it.

I enjoy showing them my inner happiness, my peace and my profound desire to love others unconditionally. I would prefer they do not have to go through all I went through to achieve it, because I see a lot of likeness with me and the youngest one. But she is the one who has to decide. And believe me, she has the patterns around her, sufficiently defined, so that she can compare between love and lack of affection, sadness and happiness, depression and energy, between health and illness. I hope she knows how to choose her path.

But if she goes wrong, I hope this book helps her so that what she has to learn is not too hard. While it is true I began to learn through my daughters what unconditional love truly is, the reality is that my biological granddaughter has ended up bringing out all the good that was hidden inside of me.

She showed me patience, tolerance, healthy 'complicity'. She helped to heal my inner child and gave me a foundation on which to start building. I can't deny that the patience and love of my daughters and husbands has given me a lot of emotional security, bringing about a change in myself. The love I profess for them inspired me to begin, but it was my granddaughter who crowned all of my efforts.

I want to contribute a little towards creating a better world for them, their descendants and the rest of humanity.

A safer world, inhabited by really happy beings,

those who with their behavior and responses to life's vicissitudes can tell you, do not despair, I am here for you. Human beings with unconditional love in their heart, being authentically happy. But, watch out! Be careful with the falsely happy one, because this also exists and, if I warn you, it is because they can confuse you and ruin everything you are trying to attain and even waste your faith in happiness.

This fake, happy person is the one who brags about his or her welfare, peace and happiness. Remember the proverb "tell me what you brag about and I will tell you what you lack." Get this person away because he or she can harm you. Normally, they are full of bitterness and they feel the need to spill out their false peace and happiness, usually to undermine your status.

However, be mindful of their attitude and copy their behavior as informative data for your course of self-transcendence, never to imitate it. That is a pattern you do not want to add to your new personality.

Always remember it is good that these people also exist because as we see them, beings weighed down by a negative load, so others see us if we adopt the same attitude. Then those people who do not know yet that they can be nicer help us – they are good teachers.

If we learn to be observant of everything and use this observation as an informative and didactic method, we will be able to turn our lives into a happy, continuous learning experience, full of satisfaction because we are collecting what we need, as tools to form our own experience. We are not registering subconsciously what we don't need. At the same time, we have our wonderful destiny in our hands. How good that is!

CHAPTER III

✳

LEARNING FROM OTHERS
"The Universe is full of teachers; let's be observant"

SOME TIME AGO, my husband told me, "since you like to read so much and practice everything you learn with yourself and others, helping people who come to you for advice, why don't you study and get certified in some career which gives you some authority to help others?"

I thought about it and began my own search. I took a course in card making which was fun; I learned how to make very fine, fretwork, repoussé invitations and congratulatory cards made in thick paper. My intention was to teach others to do this work which, besides being artistic, turned out to be good therapy.

It was not what I wanted. I started to make business cards to sell them, but I didn't find what I was looking for there either. I enrolled myself in the faculty of Public Science in the university. By that time I was really involved with a political party and I thought that could be the field where I could help others.

This turned out to be another experience, another learning situation and nothing important. My calling for service wasn't there – too materialistic and not clear enough for my sensibility. I don't want this enumeration to be too long, so I will give a little list of the steps I followed. I have several certifications and diplomas – Medical Assistant, Legal Assistant, Computer programming, Porcelanicron and Decoupage. None of these was what I wanted.

One day my young daughter invited me to a conference to be given in the university theatre. It was about Tibetan Buddhism given by two monks from Tibet about Buddhist philosophy. By that time, my daughter and I had begun to study Metaphysics and were much involved in the discovery of new truths.

We were just looking for a God who was more just and loving. I don't want to offend anybody. It is not my intention, but I'm totally convinced that punishment is a consequence of the egotism in the human mind, which is full of defects and feels it has the power to punish others.

I don't believe God is able to punish. Besides, the idea of sending you to a hell to be tortured for an eternity because you did something God did not like sounds like an act of retaliation rather than an act of justice. I believe in a loving God who gives you several opportunities for living so that you can achieve your perfection before you go back to Him; and make you a co-creator in a higher level because life goes on. It is eternal; the universe is infinite and there is a lot to create.

Remember we belong to a world of Light, not of darkness. That is my God – in that I believe and that God set me free. That time in that theatre, seeing and listening to the conference by the Tibetan monks, I witnessed the first miracle which manifested before me or at least, before my almost incredulous eyes.

A miracle is, according to the dictionary of the Spanish Language of the Royal Academy, "An inexplicable act of the natural laws attributed to the supernatural mediation of divine origin."

Of course, I believe that conception of life through a couple in each species, seeds, spores, or other means in other species is also a miracle. But this is my sentimental and spiritual appreciation because it has a scientific explanation in which I totally believe.

Besides, conception of life, being a common thing that happens thousands of times every minute, we have taken away its importance. As sensationalist beings and a little spiritually confused, we like to see something happening that with a naked eye has no human explanation. And that was what happened. During the conference about Buddhist philosophy, they invited everybody who felt moved by a true calling for service to participate in the act of initiation which was to take place.

As I previously said, I was already studying Metaphysics and I found a great similarity in both teachings. Arranged in a different manner, both disciplines teach you the achievement of unconditional love and the merit of breaking bindings so that you can keep on going on your spiritual path.

My daughter and I agreed we wanted to be initiated. Around five hundred people got up and all of us processed in front of the monks. One of them was in charge of giving us a little sip of a beverage which tasted like a wine of a very delicate flavor and the other monk gave us a red cord, a symbol of the initiation. Together, they repeated few times a mantra in the Tibetan language without stopping for a second.

But that was not all. The monk who gave me the "wine" had a small amphora, about four or five inches high, which he never refilled. This is what I mean as a miracle. Before the astonished eyes of the people there, among them, there was a representative from a prestigious newspaper in the country. Five hundred people were given "wine" to drink without refilling the amphora. What do you think? Miracle or not? For me, it was.

Because of very positive family motives, I came along with my husband and my youngest daughter to live in the United States. I continued with my spiritual studies. I prepared myself in several disciplines. I took an "Ascension" seminar which filled my life with much peace and helped me to lift myself even more to the highest with my inner spiritual power. The second seminar this was "Walking with the Angels." I took was an extraordinary experience – it is very difficult to explain you are filled with sensations when you are in front of a Pure Light Energy.

I continued preparing myself and studied the three levels of REIKI discipline and got certified as a teacher. Each learning experience has made a favorable change in me. So in order for me to be completely prepared and accredited, I enrolled myself in the university to get my degree in Metaphysics with a concentration in Spiritual Therapy.

Also, in the same university I got ordained as a Minister in Metaphysics and I added one more certification to the healing practice through the Universal Energy, by putting my hands and spiritual therapy in order to help others take out their Divine part and put it to work for their benefit.

I followed that with a doctorate in Metaphysics which reaffirmed me to give therapies at a general level and helped me in my work with children, especially with those who suffered from some psychological or physical impairment. I have never worked in a children's center; I adapted my house for my therapies and I helped some kids and their families.

Later, I worked as a teacher's assistant in an elementary school and it was there where I was able to manifest everything that I learned, supported by the very great love I've always felt for children. Somebody, whose name I do not remember, said, "It is easier to educate a child than it is to fix an adult." I add if you don't believe it, ask a professional who works with the mind.

I felt good; I was able to share my love with others through the spiritual help I provided. Somewhere I read or heard that love is the only thing that multiplies or grows when it is shared. It is true.

Some time after this my husband told me there was a company of psychics looking for people to work helping over the telephone. A fellow worker's mother-in-law told him she could help me to learn to read and interpret Tarot cards.

I went there to take classes. I told myself this could be a way to help others; I was always a mystical and religious reader; I've read and learned a lot from different religious philosophies and esotericism and I've also been involved in many religions trying to help myself so that I can help, so I thought this could be an answer. I worked on this psychic line for enough time to learn that they were dishonest people. I can't say the producers or owners of the company were cheaters because I don't have proof of that, but I am sure that many pseudo psychics abused the ignorance of spiritually and materially poor people.

I remember how I tried to help people calling for a Tarot reading to understand that if they didn't make a change in their lives; things would not improve. I offered them advice to help. Those "customers" used to tell me that what they needed was a Tarot card reading.

When I answered them that they already knew their circumstances – that paying per minute which was very expensive to listen to what they already knew was not smart, and therefore, I was offering therapeutic assistance to help them get out of that vicious circle in which they were and at the same time get out of the dependence, incredibly these callers cut off communication with me. They were trapped in the sensation produced by "the divination" of their problems.

Most of them had already spoken with other "psychics" who had collected thousands of dollars from them for doing spiritual work in them that would solve all their problems.

My God! What had I gotten into? These people did not want help; it amused them that their life circumstances were "divined", which by the way, they already knew by heart just to prove we were able to divine.

I spoke with my supervisor with whom I was a great friend or so I thought. She said she was going to deal with the situation because it was prohibited to cheat people by selling "spiritual jobs" to them, because they collect a salary for their "job."

The truth is she never did a thing and finally the psychic lines fell apart, destroyed in the way a lie is always destroyed. This can never be sustained for a long time. Honest psychics have stood on their feet – the spiritualist professionals who dedicate their life to provide true help.

I want to establish very clearly that I am not underestimating neither the religions nor the psychics or anybody who practices a spiritual philosophy with honesty because of a demand for service.

I am sure everything you visualize and create in your mind through thoughts, decrees, affirmations or rituals is going to work. I think there are people with a spiritual development, big enough to "see" or "perceive" energies and they can help very much in the growth of others.

I did find them in my life and they were really angels and beings with a lot of light. Remember this: that your life will turn into what you believe. But always make sure that what you do, or what they advise you, is full of unconditional love, that way, it does not harm you nor does it harm others.

You've got the power. This is an axiom. The positive of all this is that there are always people with a more open mind to listen with the soul's ears. When a person is receptive and your heart is filled up with love, the mind is healthy and ready to make your world perfect.

I was able to prove that a very high percentage of people who were willing to be advised and believed in themselves as the true instrument of their change, made big improvements and began to be successful in their lives, completely opposite to those who just wanted the card reading to keep repeating the same.

I began to shape what I was going to do with the abundance of true love I had found in my heart. I read the Bible again, I read several books of Metaphysics and I began to study The Kabbalah.

Perhaps it wasn't the right moment to study this discipline because three weeks after the beginning, the teacher suspended classes for reason I don't know even to this day.

I compared the Faith that the Teacher and Prophet Jesus spoke about with the affirmations which Metaphysics talks about.

Indeed, it was the same thing said in a different way. If you affirm and establish your desire as your own, no person or thing can prevent this from happening.

But, watch out! This can happen with any affirmation you make, so you must refrain from saying "I am too fat," "everything I do goes wrong," "my luck is the worst," etc. You must never affirm about your person something you do not want to get. Remember that you do not need to say the word "no" to prevent you from having something and you must never utter negative statements about something you want. To doubt a little is sufficient for not believing in it. Therefore, not obtaining what you desire is due to the fact that you denied it to yourself, nobody else did it.

MAKING CHANGES

IS THERE ANYTHING YOU want at this moment? Is your job something you do because of a vocation or a need? What you dreamed your life would be like – is that what you have now? These are a few questions you must put to yourself in order to find out whether you are on the path to success. Success is not always about money; you are really successful when you are doing what you like, and believe me, money comes when this happens. Then, why would you want to earn it doing something you dislike?

Are you merely tied to social conventions? Have you gotten obligations that are disturbing your inner peace? Do you believe your loved ones will still have all they need if you dare to follow your dreams? Well, that isn't true, I can quote some names of people who did what they liked and some who overcame great obstacles to achieve it; these people have been happy because of that.

Otherwise, they would not have achieved it. For example: philosopher, Socrates; scientist, Albert Einstein; musician, Mozart; singer, Andrea Bocelli; politician, Mahatma Ghandi. There's no one from the names mentioned above who hadn't had to overcome difficulties in order to achieve success; some of them even faced death, as long as they did what they truly desired.

And none of them would be mentioned today if they would have done what others wanted them to do. All of them had a calling for service in different professional areas, all of them dreamed about doing what they did or are doing. Socrates was sentenced to death for teaching a philosophy which at the time was accused of being corrupt. His humility made him utter his famous phrase "I just know I don't know anything." He believed that we reached the maximum scope growth through knowledge of ourselves. From there came his motto, "get to know yourself" which appears as an inscription in front of the Delphi temple.

Einstein showed so much difficulty learning in his first years of study, that his teachers came to think he suffered from mental retardation. During high school he showed interest in mathematics only. That was what he liked; he dedicated his life to science leaving a legacy to scientists and modern students of the ancient science. "Everything has a relationship, nothing is separated from anything."

Mozart was socially discriminated in France and in Paris, he endured the utmost contempt, from the noblemen whom he worked under for two years, before going back to Salzburg, his hometown.

Andrea Bocelli, who was born blind, took piano, flute and sax. He studied law at the Pisa University and after graduating as a doctor in this discipline he worked as a lawyer, elected by a tribunal. We all know his artistic achievements; he shared the stage with important figures in music all around the world.

Mohandas Karamchand Ghandi, known as Mahatma (Big Soul), also followed his dreams of a free India; he founded a movement which bears that name.

During these years, he developed an original philosophy and a method of social protest which he called satyagraha (the power of the truth or power of the soul). And he managed to influence a nation, but had to go through a lot of obstacles and fight without violence for his well deserved freedom.

This documentation is not presented with a historical, informative purpose, but rather, as examples to follow (which we all need), having as a starting point the fact that all obstacles can be overcome – you just have to believe in yourself. Remember that each obstacle is a mockery of your own negativity, labeling you useless and making fun of you.

Only you can prove you are not, only you can overcome that obstacle and prove to yourself, not to everybody else, that you are capable of achieving your goals because the barriers were broken. Actually, they were fake. And the borders? The Universe was created without borders. You are part of the Universe. Learn this and apply it.

CHAPTER IV

✴

REPROGRAMMING

THE HUMAN BODY IS a complex laboratory which, despite scientific progress, is not yet known completely, and if it is known by science, we haven't been informed of this.

What science can't deny is that this wonderful laboratory –our body, is ruled by the biggest employer in the world. But be careful, this employer is not autonomous; it works by programming. I'm talking about our mind. Each time science boasts about some discovery, the mind registers new information and adds its own ramifications to this discovery; becoming a difficult adversary to overcome.

Disease has been the challenge which science has managed to sleep, but not to defeat. Death is the enemy science will never defeat with its laboratory instruments. Why? Because science, being able to walk hand in hand with Spiritual Life, has refused to befriend it.

Haven't you noticed that science and the Universal Energy are considered the same thing, and if you have, you know that ego has been valued above love for humanity? This ego has individualized to such an extent, that each one wants to possess its own accomplishments.

An entity that just looks for its own benefit will never be able to achieve perfection or overcome that which until now has been undefeatable--disease. But, where does disease come from?

Why does it have so much destructive power? What is it doing, cohabiting with beings who were created healthy and perfect, and to be happy? Is it perhaps that the Universal Power gloats in seeing us beaten down, begging for a miracle which doesn't come? Or are we asking on our knees for the solution to a situation that seems to worsen with our cries?

What happens is that when we get desperate and beg, we are subdued by the pressure of a negative energy which doesn't allow generating light to act in order to resolve the problem.

It is not easy to change the programming of several lifetimes, so my advice is to proceed gradually. The good thing is that no matter how small our change may be the positive consequences are great.

Most human beings are able to forgive a small injustice. Just as a percentage boasts about forgiving a little, there's another group, the most dangerous (because the worst enemy is the hypocrite), who says he forgives and forgets, but does neither. Bitterness sets in and we remember the offence at the first opportunity. Why is this? We were taught as children that the ultimate authority in forgiveness is God. He gives us one life only--very hard by the way—and demands that we become perfect for Him, while putting obstacles in the way of our saintliness, and if we do not succeed he gives us a horrific and sadistic punishment. From where then, do we learn this bitterness? What can we do to begin the process of learning to forgive?

I'm going to teach you how I did it. I always emphasize in my teachings that I'm still human, that this is day – to – day work. But I also want you to know that I'm a better human being, that I love God-- I don't fear Him. I don't improve the quality of my spiritual being to avoid going to hell, but out of free choice and the unconditional love which I've developed for my neighbor. Through a lot of work, I've learned to love the one who harms and hurts me.

I've managed to prove to myself that it can be done and this is what I wish for you. At the end of this book you'll find the steps I followed which will help you accomplish everything you want. You will also find my postal address and if you need help, you'll find my arms open, full of unconditional love for you.

IMAGE AND LIKENESS

"SO GOD CREATED MAN in His own image, in the image of God He created him; male and female created He them." Gen. 1:27 Well, if you pay a little attention to this, it is logical to understand that if God is a Spiritual Being, an Energy of Light, a Universal Brain, the Generating Omniscient Mind and not a Physical Being visible to the human eye, our human inheritance must also be spiritual, energetic, and super-intelligent, co-creating throughout the Universe.

Everything reproduces according to its kind. Cows do not have chickens, but calves; hens get chicks from their eggs and not little goats and so on and so forth through a natural process. All that gets reproduced is according to its kind, as that Wonderful Creating Energy not only Creates, but maintains an Order.

Look around you and you will see order in all creation. It's logical to think that if we're God's children, we are little gods with all the creating power over our own universe.

This universe involves our body, the environment, quality of life, personal circumstances and everything that concerns our human life, including all kinds of problems and circumstances.

If this is so, why the crying and the sacrifice? Could you imagine God saying: "Please universe, be created. Animals, could you please show yourselves? Man I beg you, make yourself like me, I need you." It sounds a little absurd, doesn't it? Rather ridiculous.

All you have to do is begin with your real self (your spiritual being) and begin to work with your environment through Him. Many people still prefer to fill their emptiness through religion. It's not a bad thing, but I'm certain it's extremely slow. With all due respect, most of the religions have delayed man's evolution by nullifying his free will and planting fear of future punishment that doesn't exist. Which of you would burn your child for disobeying?

Well, this is homework for you. If you feel a little afraid in not attending church anymore, start asking why are you afraid. If God is a source of security, a giver of material and spiritual provisions, then something must be wrong. But even so, you can begin your change by going to the church of your choice. What I'm trying to teach here doesn't fit with any religious doctrine; on the contrary, I'm going to teach you easy steps which will help you develop unconditional love and forgiveness.

What is going to happen without a doubt is that little by little, you will realize your life changes-- in some cases, changes can be seen instantly.

But what changes will be manifested? Although it seems incredible to you, these will be in every aspect of your life, believe me.

Notice that creation is always mentioned in the singular- –never is it called creations. It is One-- His Child. The universe with all its contents, including several universes very similar to ours with different kinds of life, is His Child and you are part of it; therefore, what I accomplish, you do too, because we are the same energy with the same wonderful inheritance. A loving Father made His testament in our favor and left us His Legacy in life. Because of this I can assure you, The Universe, The Generating Energy, The Universal Brain, God, will never die. Therefore we will never die either.

THE CHILDREN

FOR YEARS I'VE WORKED with children. I love them. I like their sincerity, their straightforward love and their expert way of teaching us. Most of us think that children are little and useless human beings whose lives we have to rule. We overprotect and manipulate them; we punish them just for being who they are. We end up castrating them emotionally and intellectually to get them to be what we want, or in order for them to become what we wanted to be and didn't dare so as not to challenge our "parents" – sorry, I mean our parents.

I am convinced that children are capable beings who are also self–sufficient. When they start to walk they keep falling until they can stand up by themselves – they don't need us for that. All of their development is in the same manner; we must only help and protect them when they ask, or else we are putting obstacles in their way. When they were born they already had their personality; they already were themselves. In other words, their talent and calling came with them; it is not something to be decided later. And whatever their calling or personality is, a child must feel he is loved, admired, accepted, and unique.

This book is very far from being about children; but I want to emphasize the things I learned from children who have helped me and keep helping me on my path.

This Christmas, a girl told me her grandmother

spent a lot of money to send her an expensive present. I think this is the message they gave the child—that her grandmother, an elderly woman had made a great, sacrificial effort, going to the post office in the cold winter to show how much she loved her granddaughter. This is what I call wrong data processing; and that someone who truly loves children, would call "child abuse."

Yes, because abuse is not just beating up a child or being sadistic in a psychological manner. Teaching them from when they are little that love has a material value is a crime that will result in a lot of trauma and neurotic needs when they become adults – needs and trauma which will lead to visits to the psychologist, for the most intelligent ones. These are the ones who realize their life can be happy and prosperous – independent of material things – on both a physical and psychological level. And there are those who don't realize they could have a good life. Dependence is not good and the only difference between dependence on one thing or another is that some are legal and others are not.

They are equally harmful ways of being. Both of them turn us into useless entities, incapable of surviving in a world full of complexity and competitiveness.

Not too long ago, a girl from the center I worked for told me, "You've told me you love me many times and I've never told you I love you. Today I want to give you this picture I did for my mother so that you know I also love you very much."

It is almost impossible to describe the different emotions that I felt. Her words were not said out of obligation. She knew I loved her and even though she would never have told me, when she did, it wasn't to take advantage. That is the difference between a child and an adult.

Usually, the child doesn't do things out of self- interest. The child who is self-seeking has been taught this at home. Most children learn to take advantage from the "business deals" their parents transact with them. I know some parents who blackmail their daughter every day. They give her the message that public schools are bad and that if she gets bad grades, they're going to get her out of the private collegiate where she studies and move her to a public one.

The message this girl receives is confusing. "If the public school is bad, why are they going to enroll me there? Do my parents love me? Or do they just love me if I get good grades?" Of course this girl is getting a wrong message about love.

It would be different if she was told, "Your responsibility as a daughter is to study so that you can have the power to choose when you become an adult and to get ready to live in a society which is very competitive. We in turn will back you up in everything – as our finances permit – until you have a profession. You are in a private school because we think is the best for you, but this is expensive and that is why we ask you to take advantage of this opportunity. We love you and trust in your ability to move forward." I am sure that ninety – five percent of this girl's reaction would be positive. Otherwise, this girl is going to do exactly what her parents want her to do – she'll acquire good grades in exchange for a gift, a trip, a tour or for being able to stay at the expensive college.

But, love will not be in what she does. She'll be

like that as an adult. She'll look for a job that pays well even though she feels unhappy; that is what she's been programmed for.

Don't offer a prize for studying hard or good grades; this isn't right. Instead, give something to your child without a motive and tell them that when you went into the store you saw something that would be a nice present for them. Don't even tell them that you bought it because you love them; for then the message would be that love is demonstrated with presents.

Another experience-- very negative by the way-- is about of a mother who goes to the center where I worked and brings her daughter, the lady has always shown an arrogant and proud attitude and she keeps humiliating people who allow themselves to be humiliated.

My co-workers avoided her, criticizee her and didn't like her. The girl was lonely in the beginning and wouldn't relate with the other children. I thought that perhaps it was the product of her mother's lack of loving words to her, because I never saw her saying goodbye with the love and tenderness other parents showed to their kids there. So I dedicated myself to give the girl special attention until she gained trust in me, in the place, and in herself.

The five-year old girl had already made some friends and she related to all of them in a good way until one day I told her we couldn't go beyond the area which was safe for her, to go into that area she needed to be older.

The mother complained that my attitude showed bad manners. The poor lady (because this kind of person deserves pity) advised the girl to tell me she was going to go where she liked and that I didn't have the right to take her out of the older children area, mother had received permission from upper management and used that against the actual rules I was supposed to follow.

The girl was never told that at the request of many parents and the personnel—including myself – who worked in the children's area, changes had been made so that five year old children were allowed in that area. What a wrong message was planted in that little girl's mind.

This angel, only five years old, is already prepared to humiliate others and will be an unpleasant person just like her mother, unless, when she grows up, she looks for help to change her bad programming.

Another mistaken teaching this innocent girl kept in her memory was that if you have a relationship with people in charge at the place you attend, you can break rules which others are not allowed to break.

But, how can I help to change this? Only in this manner—by asking parents who are reading this book to care for their children's mental health, not to be what we don't want them to be, to watch what we say and do in front of them and to let them be. Not in vain the Teacher of Teachers said, "Be like little children." Let us not poison our children so they can continue to be pure, even after being adults.

When I speak about purity, I mean their mind and their heart. Well, the equation is made: CHWS = UAA, this is, Children without Suffering equals Useful Adapted Adults. All our bad or good programming begins in our mother's womb. But what is the purpose of blaming our parents if it has been negative? That isn't a remedy for the situation on the contrary, it worsens it. Ninety- nine per cent of parents love their children, and while they are being raised, if there is bad programming (and there's bound to be) it's because we think we're doing the best thing.—We either copy from our parents or else we lack psychological-spiritual knowledge to provide the solid base we don't ourselves possess. Something I learned working on a psychic line was how insecure people are. How are we going to get our children ready if we are not prepared? How can we help them if we must look for help for ourselves? I am not talking about people of little learning. During the time I offered spiritual help I met humble people with very little education, middle-class people with more education and professionals with an apparent intellectual capability.

In my house I have received people of considerable culture and some very rich ladies, worried about their mates. Where are they from? I've been consulted by Arabians, Americans, Central and South Americans, Europeans and others who belong to some of the best-known religions. What happens? Why the insecurity? We go back to the same thing. Dependence and insecurity were developed in our mother's womb, and are due to different factors. Don't ask somebody else to solve what only you can solve. Don't ask other people for an answer for your circumstances. Look for your inner "I" and dialogue with him or her. Only you know what you want; therefore, only you can satisfy your longing.

Money? This is just one of the many instruments we count on to satisfy some of these wishes. The rest you accomplish with struggle and firmness, with a youthful spirit, with a child's heart and with all the love in the world inside it.

But remember, love must be unconditional. Do you think it doesn't work? Give it a try; it's completely free. I promise your life will change.

CHAPTER V

✳

CLEANSE YOUR SOUL

I HAVE SPOKEN WITH many people about forgiveness. All of them begin by saying they know how to forgive, that they have done so in the worst cases of their lives. When we go deeper into their feelings, bitterness emerges, with its painful memories and the usual blaming of others. Most of them have ended up admitting that these feelings are as real and as poignant as they were the day it happened. Human suffering – most of the time or we could say, always – yields to a masochistic feeling which we do not want to admit.

The process in the human ego works in us and we don't notice it; we don't want to admit our guilt and mistakes. Nor are we capable of accepting that what happens is just the result of some mistake, whether or not we did it on purpose.

There is always a consequence of our energy imbalance. Although it doesn't always show right away – and even if this were the case, we don't admit it – the truth of the matter is we create each circumstance of our life and bitterness brings a great portion of guilt, along with envy.

We're going to learn in this chapter to reprogram ourselves so we can forgive. This is a daily job and requires an affirmation you do with both your mind and your heart.

Remember, your mind is not autonomous; it sends you previously recorded messages, received by you or by others. It doesn't make a decision on its own despite the power conferred on it, and despite the sleepless nights it produces. It can't do it by itself; you authorize it, you program it and it delivers you back its programming. It has no power. You give the mind its power.

If every day, you use an affirmation of forgiveness and repeat it before going to sleep, fully conscious of what you are saying and with a sincere desire, the day will come when you can forgive the biggest injustices and damages committed against you. You can even forgive the horrendous crimes being committed against humanity, animals and the environment, throughout the planet. You must first realize the universal communion in your mind.

You must learn that you are not an entity apart from the rest of creation, that what you are going through, each of us is also going through, that we all struggle to be better human beings, that we all want to be happy and prosperous.

When I talk about spirituality, the creation and the universe, I am not preaching. Nothing is farther from my mind. I want to get to the heart of all those who suffer, all those who think their luck is over. Unfortunately, faith is so divided you can't make it through preaching religion, because religion, which means "to tie again," has been responsible for putting nations and kingdoms against each other. And it goes further; Religion is separating – in other words "untying" – the family.

I just ask you to believe in yourself. If you do it, you already believe in God, in whichever way you conceive God and whatever name you call Him.

He will always be the Generating Energy of each life. If you start believing in yourself, almost without realizing it, you'll begin to notice that a door you never imagined will open. People begin seeing you in another light. That person, considered incapable – somewhat useless – begins to transform into a useful being who does admirable things.

Then come that love and respect for yourself that lets you be where you want to be. You do what you want to do and, as a result, you get a job which makes you happy and furthermore, you get paid for it. What I'm saying is not a fairy tale. It has happened to me and to millions in the world.

If you are a regular reader, you have read many books by people who narrate their experiences; people like you and me, who one day said, "It's enough! Life can't be like this; nor can the purpose of Creation." And when I talk about Creation I do it in the true sense of the word, whether you believe in the Bible creation or in the Big Bang. I'm talking about the generating principle – where we come from, how we began.

It doesn't matter what you believe in. There was nobility in the Universal purpose to desire our existence – therefore, we can't fail. We are superior, capable, and totally and absolutely perfect in our spiritual or energetic inheritance.

Do you follow me? Do you realize that that person with a fatigued look, unhappy and complaining about getting up out of bed everyday, is not you?

So, in the same way, neither is the person who is dependent, the person he should be. I'm going to tell you a story. A lady got divorced from a man who annoyed and humiliated her more than you can imagine. Let's call them Mrs. Vela and Mr. Marquez. This man left her and went to live a crazy life, but got sick. He was about to die and this woman took him into her home and offered him a guest room. You're probably thinking the same as I thought at the beginning – what a good heart; what a wonderful work of forgiveness.

But the following years showed that she was using him. She never got used to loneliness and feels socially embarrassed to be divorced, so she uses him as a chauffeur for her trips on the road, and he feels obligated to share and stay with her family on those trips. She makes him feel guilty if he decides to be with his children at Christmas. She uses him to do the things she doesn't want to do and to take care of her businesses when she has to travel. In exchange, she lends him money which he, because he is already retired, can't pay back – with the little jobs he gets here and there – and which keeps him obligated to live with her.

Using her feminine tactics and her mother's illness as an excuse, she has separated him from his family. What happens? While she makes her family, friends and clients believe they are a couple again, the truth is that in the center of their lives, there's no mutual respect.

This man, tied to a computer, is still having the same conquests which humiliated her before. He still says the same things he used to say and keeps putting her through the same heartache.

Mrs. Vela, far from being a Good Samaritan, is a poor woman full of complexities, which make her a failure to herself. Her lack of self esteem and dignity has made her dependent on a man who is even thinking of living elsewhere. He has bought a property but doesn't know how to move out because he feels he is morally obligated to Mrs. Vela.

Mr. Marquez is also failing himself and complains he always has to please everybody else. Here you have two cases of no self-respect. Both of them are throwing out the dignity they talk about so much. She should become mentally free from a man's dependency, a man who feels pity for her. He must change his pity to self esteem and make the life he feels like having.

Being grateful does not mean owing your life to somebody. Whoever does you a favor and wants you to pay for it in some way, isn't doing you a favor; consciously or unconsciously he wants to tie you up. He feels he has bought you.

I'm going to teach you something that did me good and continues to do so – how to forgive and get untied. In order to forgive, you don't have to go back to the person who humiliated, harmed and mistreated you. This can become a sado-masochistic situation like in Mrs. Vela and Mr. Marquez' case. You can, in some instances, keep a good friendship or a measure of cordiality.

But, watch out! Sometimes the act of going back gives opportunity for the same errors to be repeated, and rage and bitterness grow. You must be careful. Working to make changes may last a lifetime. The good thing is that improvement manifests promptly.

I tell this little story with the purpose of getting us to observe our motivation. When we do a favor we must be sure the person doesn't feel tied to us, nevertheless, we should not be annoyed because that person can't respond, the moment we need it.

This happened to me on one occasion, with a very close person, whom I love profoundly. This person did me a favor in a difficult time. In two months she needed help and I couldn't give it. Only I knew, in the deepest part of me, how painful it was for me to be unable to reciprocate.

The good thing is that although we have limits, God doesn't. I am sure He will respond to this person in some manner and even in other circumstances, because The Light always rewards the cheerful giver. This shouldn't present the smallest doubt for anybody. I make this clear because in the tale of Mrs. Vela and Mr. Marquez, she could have been taking revenge, but it's possible she didn't even realize how costly his favors were.

Let's be alert when giving because this must be forgotten in the same way as the offenses that were done to us. It is not nice to tell someone you have helped that you've always been there when they need you. Your right hand must ignore what the left hand gives and vice versa. Or else, you are humiliating the person and all the good you did, gets lost.

AFFIRMATION

An effective rule to forgive and be forgiven

If in any place of the Universe there is a cell
-physical or in the form of energy-
that needs my forgiveness; I send it with unconditional love from my heart.
I forgive myself for the harm I might have done,
consciously or unconsciously to any kind of life
on the planet.
I forgive myself for loving me so little, that I
allowed others to hurt me.
I ask The Generating Energy to forgive each life,
for me and for my neighbor.
I thank you Father-Mother because I know you
heard me.

CHAPTER VI

I WANT AND I CAN

IN MY PRACTICE AS a therapist I've heard it all. The majority of people used to tell me that they had lost their faith in prayer. Of course, at this point in the book, we know the only thing they never had was faith in themselves. No prayer works without a great portion of faith.

Faith has many definitions, but all of them imply faith, one way or another, in something or somebody. When I was a girl I was taught in the Catholic religion, because I studied in a nuns' college. Faith is to believe in what we don't see. According to the Spanish language, in regard to one of many definitions of faith, it is security, the assertion of something being true. So, one way or another, you must take for granted or believe that what you have asked for was given to you so that it can be manifested.

It is through faith that a miracle is performed. This is not a magic act, but an act of faith. Prayers are not to be liturgically repeated without getting at the essence, because your conscious mind does not record what you say.

You must, without forcing yourself, pay attention to what you are saying. The circumstance is as follows: you, just like the famous doll who kept all of her husband's belongings, brought all your belongings when you were born. You just have to be sure that they get manifested. There are no privileged beings on the planet Earth; there are beings who don't know their privileges and therefore, they are not enjoying them. Many people, whom I had the opportunity to talk to, lacked self esteem.

All of them, one way or another, thought the rest had a better job, that their husband was unfaithful, that their children were worse than their friends' or neighbors' children, that they were fat, or they had thin legs, etc. There are a lot of attachments people place on themselves, preventing the freeing of their spirit and receiving their reward. Do you remember what the Teacher Jesus used to do before performing a miracle?

He'd say the grace in advance: "Father, I thank thee that thou hast heard me, and I know thou hearest me always." He did it when raising Lazarus from his tomb and every time He performed a miracle, He'd say thank you before seeing it. What is that? FAITH.

So then, understand, faith doesn't admit failures. If you want something which, by the Divine Law belongs to you, do not beg, don't go beating around the bush saying, "Please little God, give me this or that." I've heard them and I know what they say. The truth is that everything is already given; Creation, in whichever way, has already been manifested; it already exists, therefore all is given already. If you ask you are affirming you don't have – therefore, you aren't going to receive.

The perfect prayer must be that which manifests your desire to receive what belongs to you. Instead of saying "God, please I need a new car," you could change it to "Father, I know my new car is some place, I thank you for that," and simply be sure it is yours already.

In regard to the sick, even though you see the person in a grave condition, say the following, "Thank you Father-Mother God for your presence in this circumstance; I declare health and life in this situation." But don't just do it with the ones you know and love. I say it each time I see an accident on the highway or an ambulance, also when somebody talks in front of me about a sick person.

We have to declare health and life for everybody, not only for the ones we love.

The problem many people have is fear to change their traditional way of seeing God.

He-She, Father-Mother God, life's Universal Generating Energy, is not an ogre who is going to punish you for your failures. Whoever lives in fear can't improve because he is just obeying through fear of punishment and feels obligated to follow a pattern, colored by his particular religion. And the highly-acclaimed free will? It is fine, thanks!

When you are a baby you make an enormous effort to sit down for the first time, then you start to crawl. Later on you achieve a great feat of your early childhood – the ability to stand up. You look at everybody with a big smile because in spite of being a baby, you know you have taken a big step in your growth – you've stood up with no help.

But, what happens? Well, your bones are still very new and your mind is beginning to develop your balance, and bang! You fall down. Have you seen a mother severely punish her baby because he fell down?

Then later, you keep going in your growth process and you become a daredevil under the loving supervision of the maternal or paternal eye. There's no punishment here, just laughs and happiness.

But what happens when you've finished growing? Well, things have changed a little; they punish you when you do certain things. Of course, being punished by others is a human concept, not a divine one. Our parents don't allow us to learn from mistakes; they punish us so that we learn and, what do they get? The most courageous of us pay no attention to them and repeat the same mistakes. We who are cowards are afraid of them.

But even so, I haven't met parents with a sound mind who burn their child's hand for breaking the rules, whatever these may be. A good parent suffers when he punishes his offspring.

Are we superior, then, to God? Why must He use eternal punishment? At this stage of the evolution of the human mind, where we fight for the protection of animals and the environment, where people have awakened or are waking up to unconditional love, which is manifested in non-discrimination and the protection of life, doesn't it seem to be a barbaric act? A useless act of revenge?

Yes, revenge, because supposedly, the purpose of punishment is correction, a call to serenity and common sense. If the punishment is eternal, it's not correction but vengeance -retaliation.

No, The Creating Energy or God doesn't do those things, so start using your faith in your favor. Begin feeling like a baby of the universe whom his Celestial Parents see with a smile and love each time he falls and tries to get up again until finally, he manages to stay on his feet. This will give you, just like me, the satisfaction of truly loving your Divine source, not fearing It.

But don't forget there's a consequence for everything you do, think, or say. Certainly, that is the way you learn as you go, the way to receive the lessons you give to yourself through the things you bring about.

This is cause and effect, or as the Teacher Jesus said, "For all they that take the sword, shall perish with the sword." So think positively, act positively, talk positively and please, look at the results all around you; they'll enchant you. Laugh constantly – there are scientific proofs about laughter being a healer. It cures. So then, change tears for laughter, hardships for gladness, wailing for joyful music, and cast your hardships to the wind.

THE PERFECT PRAYER

I know I am a sparkle of the Great Central Sun,
A perfect cell of the Creating Energy.
As such, I am also a creator, because
I inherit the power of Him, whose seed I am.
By the power obtained within the pale of The Light,
I decree for my life the following:
I'm physically, mentally and spiritually healthy;
I'm a giver of light and unconditional love;
I'm a millionaire in love, health, gladness and
Money; I own everything that exists in the universe.
My home is as big as the one of my
Heavenly Parents.
My loved ones are protected by the Divine
Light and I rest upon the assurance that they,
My neighbor and I will always be covered,
And we will receive all of what we accept to receive.
Amen

CHANGE DOES NOT HURT

WHEN YOU MAKE THE decision to make a change in your life for the first time, you're afraid. It's like going to the doctor or the dentist. In a way it is, but this time you'll be your own doctor, and it's only you who is in charge of the healthy medicine of forgiveness to begin your healing.

A woman customer of mine once told me, "I try to forgive her, but every time I see her cynical face I feel this rage." There is the problem or the circumstance, but don't try to recreate that person's face in your mind. Do what is possible to keep her away from you; make drastic changes if you have to, but do not allow anything to interrupt your healing process. Don't place obstacles on your path to prevent making a change in your life. It's your mental and spiritual health which is at stake – your happiness and ultimately, your life.

Yes, most people end up getting sick from so much bitterness. There are doctors who admit that rage, envy, and negative feelings of all kinds are devastating to human health. In a body ruled by a positive mind, illness can remain dormant, without any trace of symptoms. Many autopsies have revealed not only a grave illness which never developed, but persons who possibly lived many years with an illness, without even knowing about it, because it never developed to the point of undermining that person.

According to the author from whom I got this information, statistics show that all these people were of excellent character, and in one way or another practiced community service because of the love in their hearts. This could have been the reason they always manifested good health.

There is an excellent book listed in my anthology, which I recommend, as it mentions something we never think about.

The heart is the main vehicle of love and good emotions; it's also the only organ that doesn't get sick with cancer. Does it have a relationship with love? Well, it would be good to think about this and come to some conclusion.

There is a prayer that helped me at the start of my accomplishments; yes, the change began long before. It is a prayer I meticulously wrote, thinking of all I had learned in the books, in my practice and from other sources.

The purpose of this prayer is to reprogram my mind, trying to replace the old and archaic programming, and which I repeat every night before sleeping. It is composed of several affirmations.

Each affirmation touches a key point and guides the part of the brain which affects that area of our life. Once programmed, it's a matter of keeping the programming rhythm active. This way, every time you're waiting for a situation to happen, your brain sends you the message that what you are looking for is there.

Or, otherwise it sends you to the place where you are able to receive it. Have you ever heard somebody say, "It was a matter of luck; I was in the right place, at the right time?"

Of course this example is applicable to positive

programming. When we deal with negative progra-mming, we have the case of the person who spends his or her life talking about tragedies and violence, assured that he or she can't leave the house because he's terrified by the street crime and feels his life is at risk. The situation and of course, the final outcome, are different.

This person goes out as usual, but this time, he finds theirself involved in a shooting and dies, a victim of a stray bullet. The final comment is, "Poor soul, that person was at the wrong place, at the wrong time."

Believe me, nothing is the product of chance or causality. Poverty of life is asked for, the same as pros-perity. You choose what you desire for your life. Albert Einstein said, "We'll have the destiny we have deser-ved." Jesus affirmed that, "For all they that take the sword shall perish with the sword." "Be careful with the bonfire you light against your enemy, you may scorch yourself." – a quote by William Shakespeare. Three people from three different ages; a scientist, a teacher, and a playwright, all in agreement.

You and nobody else can make the change, if you are battling with the truth and the light, believe me, you'll have a great challenge to reach your goal. Truth and light go hand in hand; whoever looks for truth, finally finds the Light.

And what is truth? Well, it is simply "you." You can't spend life copying, when you have your own wonderful genetic map, and it doesn't matter if there is a physical impediment. Remember, it's only physical.

You are still mentally, spiritually and energetically powerful, and invincible. Your dreams belong to you; therefore, only you can accomplish them. Give yourself a gift of love, begin being you, strengthen your energy from the inside, with all the faith you can. I was talking to a friend who told me, "Well, perhaps not everybody who reads your book wants to make a change in his life."

It's a good thing he told me that because he made me remember there's something I haven't clarified. I don't write this with the intention of attacking anyone, or making them feel obligated. This literature is directed to those who still believe they can't make a drastic change in their life; yet, they fervently desire it in their deepest self. My book is not directed to those who deny themselves and get old waiting for an opportunity; but rather to those who know from the inside, that opportunity is here and now.

Remembering the past and planning the future, a beautiful present which we don't enjoy, escapes us. And what is the future? Nothing but the tomorrow of today. Yesterday may be full of achievements with beautiful memories –but that was yesterday. Those are memories – only memories. When I talk about fighting to accomplish something, I'm aware that there are limitations which can cause impediments. Although the will breaks obstacles, I can't pretend everybody thinks alike.

For example, if the dream of your life was to be an Olympic champion, but this book comes to your hands when you are eighty years old, I suggest you consider the challenge you have in front of you, before taking it up. Not because I doubt you can do it, but because you're going to encounter more obstacles than when you were twenty-five. Mexico has a runner who sold newspapers all of her life. She did the deliveries running; she did that for years until one day somebody proposed that she run professionally. She believed in herself; this is not common.

But, why did she accomplish it? Simply, she believed in herself. While it's a great stimulus when others believe in us and praise us for our helpful work, it's true that if we don't believe in ourselves, it doesn't matter what others believe.

Do you know who I am talking about? Of all the six thousands athletes who competed in the World's Veterans Athletics; Rosario Iglesias, at the age of 95 was the indisputable star. She won the gold in both the 100 and 200 meter race. My respect and unconditional love go to Chayito.

Going back to you who are reading this book at the age of eighty-five and want to make it real within the field that excites you, but you do not want to conquer the obstacles which your mental age imposes, you could write a column about sports in a magazine or a book about topics that sports lovers would like to read.

Notice I've written "mental age." That's because I just gave an example of where there is no impediment if the energy is healthy. In this very changed world, where the mass media enters your home, basically without asking permission, I think that even the "Chinese from Borneo" know about the successful people in their world who are handicapped. There are famous singers who are blind and painters who do marvelous works with their feet because they have no arms.

Not long ago, on a well -known Hispanic television program, I saw an interview with a beautiful and happy Hispanic woman who had no arms. This lady gave a beautiful smile to the public and then she sat down to greet them with her feet, with as much skill as we, who have hands, would use in our hand gestures.

Then, a few days later I received a video through my computer where a pretty and young North American mother dressed and caressed her baby only a few months old with her feet. She didn't have arms either.

There are many stories which all of you have heard, and which perhaps you don't pay attention to, other than at the moment you see them. Remember, there are teachers everywhere and in all the types of creation, not just among human beings. Observe the animals and also, the plants and you know what? They don't have to read a book. They are guided by that energy I was talking to you about at the beginning of the book, which all of us possess, as well. The Energy of the Source. We are His Seed. Let us then germinate and produce beautiful fruit.

CHAPTER VII

✳

SEARCHING MYSELF

WHEN I WAS A little girl I used to play hide and seek at school and on the patio at home, with my sisters and friends. It was fun, especially when we found the perfect hiding place. It seems that we do the same thing with ourselves. Each time our existence deserves a change, we hide from ourselves behind that which we've already accomplished.

In a conversation with a person who feels it is not the time to make changes, I heard him saying he feels free, nobody has ever tied him down, nor ever will, and that he's always done what he wanted, while everyone around him keeps doing the same thing. Ever since I've known this person he's been a salesperson. He first worked in a clothing store, for others, and later he owned several shops. What for? To provide others with a service.

I don't think it's bad, but can he say it's others who have always done the same, when the same thing in his life has been repeated for years? I believe in success, but I learn from failure. The person, who keeps saying that he does as he pleases and that this is not the time to change, is probably the person who needs more change in its life.

It's like the one who tells you about the wonders in his or her home, his career, children, and the perfect and happy life he or she has. What's in sight doesn't need the help of eyeglasses. Again, the proverb states, "Tell me what you brag about and I'll tell you what you lack." To pretend we have a perfect life on this planet is something nobody is going to believe. Please don't say it. Yes, you can be happy most of the time. Yes, you can learn to break through the pain and understand that if it has a solution, there's no reason to suffer and if there is no solution there can be less suffering. Yes, you can have a prosperous life and help others to improve their self-esteem so that their lives also improve.

Yes, in fact you can become immensely rich – mentally, spiritually and materially. But, keeping peace and the planet's happiness for yourself? Please, don't fool yourself because a liar falls before the crippled. This life is not about competition; you don't want your neighbor as an opponent. We don't want to fight to be better than others. Life is about all of us being better. It is about doing, serving, and loving so intensely, that we come to feel authentically happy with others' happiness.

THOUGHT

If just a moment I spent thinking;
not leaving my mind spills out by itself,
when freeing my dreams I'd be gaining
all the sea's power, in a wave.

AFFIRMATION FOR PROSPERITY.

I am a spiritual being, full of light and love
I belong to the Heavenly Dynasty,
I've got an immense power over my environment
and a degree in the architecture of my destiny.
As a divine energy I own the power to change my
life and build my bliss. I am a giver of light and
unconditional love.
Nothing can make my life's water muddy, I am
healthy, a transmitter of peace; my hands offer,
never take away. By all the power I inherit, and
lives inside of me, I decree that:
I am prosperous because together with all the
Creation I am co-owner of the universe, I am rich
according to the measure and capacity for which
material riches I am prepared for; I am open to
keep receiving prosperity blessings, health, light
and love for me and for the rest of the Creation.
Thank you.

ENCOUNTERING OURSELVES

IN ORDER TO FIND ourselves, we have to mentally go back to childhood. We were not malicious and looked for the most foolish places to hide. For example, behind a tree which was two feet away from the girl or boy who was counting up to ten or twenty?

When we're searching inside, we don't have to go very deep. We don't have to go far in the memory, or feel we're going crazy trying to find our true personality; it is there less than two feet away. Close your eyes, empty your mind from everything it's full of – today.

Look at yourself. There you are a little afraid, but with great desire to let yourself out. Come on, greet yourself, and welcome yourself. It's you – such as you were conceived in the womb of the Creating Energy, with all your virtues, your authentic happiness and with your talent or calling.

There, where you find yourself, is your baggage. You came with all that is necessary to evolve, with joy and satisfaction. So, take your suitcase which is full of dreams, goals, gladness, accomplishments, satisfactions and a big dose of Divine Energy to fertilize them; and thus, your attainment tree will grow.

Now, don't expect you're going to find yourself tonight, and tomorrow when you get up, the tree of your complete realization is going to be there, upright, leafy and producing fruit. That isn't true.

You've got the materials and must begin to build;

the time it takes you depends on the persistence you have while building.

I've always thought that, as the architects puts a deadline on his work, and makes a contract with a company to deliver the building material, the constructor of his or her life must do the same.

In this way you have in your mind an idea of the time your masterpiece, YOU, are going to take to materialize.

Take all those materials you brought with you, and those which are being born during your process of change, and start shaping what you want. The choice of how to use them and how not to use them is yours; the consequences either good or bad, will also be in your hands.

Inside your luggage, there are some other products and building materials, which could be called destructive materials -such as envy, hate, selfishness, bitterness, gossip and a lot more of all kinds of little stones.

You must know how to build a good foundation with the right materials, and begin discarding those that stuck to your luggage in your journey through the universe, when you undertook your way from Our Heavenly Home, to the Earth. A German philosopher by the name of Arthur Schopenhauer said, "Friends are considered to be sincere; enemies really are. For this reason it is advisable to take advantage of all their censorship to get to know ourselves a little better. It is somewhat like taking a bitter medicine."

From a metaphysical point of view and according to a psychoanalyst, whom I consulted in this matter, your enemy is not really telling you the whole truth.

There can be envious feelings involved, but given that we attract people who have some of our own peculiarities, we can take note of all that that person says about our own person, because that means he or she is suffering from those same defects and negative qualities which afflict us to some degree.

Do I make myself clear? If somebody calls you envious, it's because that person is envious. The Teacher of teachers and the greatest Prophet that ever set foot on our planet said, "Not that which goeth into the mouth defileth a man; but that which cometh out of the mouth, this defileth a man." (Matt. 15, 11).

It would be good if some sectors of the medical profession gave this some thought. How is it possible that this has not evolved yet, in the way they treat an ill person? It is about time that, instead of bombarding you with drugs and chemicals -with warnings in tiny print—that in order to relieve your symptoms (not cure you), you may get kidney disease, dizziness, insomnia and perhaps even breathing problems. Or they prescribe hormones and contraceptives which could give you cancer. They might have said to you, "We are going to change your diet, but this must be accompanied by a change in your customs and ways of seeing life."

Thank God, there are already many doctors who are doing this. Human life can't nor should depend on another person or the time that an insurance company (who are really directing everything) allows a doctor to see you for a medical visit.

We must confront the cause, not the effect. Heal your soul, stop living with fears and forget the foolishness of eternal punishment.

Clean your heart and love unconditionally; learn to forgive. "Sin" doesn't enter a heart full of love. Be authentically happy. When you learn this, try to spread this happiness to others. It's not that you're making others happy – this isn't possible, although many believe it is. Others notice your change *energetically*, and begin to make their own change. Happiness is contagious. We can help without pushing. Nobody can be obligated to change, because not even your shoes can be put on by force. Be and let them be.

Each person is and must feel responsible for what happens to them; it's the only way to be acknowledged before the universe, who created them. If you interfere even with just some advice, when something is wrong the universe will blame you. The human being always looks for someone to blame, and therefore change is hard for humans. You just reflect your light, and automatically others will feel illuminated by it.

A few days ago, a co-worker asked me for advice. She suffers from psoriasis which has covered almost all her body. She always wears long pants and long-sleeved blouses.

I suggested that she cleanse her organism and start a detoxification diet, involving a few changes in her eating.

For this, according to my criteria, she must go to a naturopathic doctor. The first thing she told me was the following, "Don't tell me I have to quit eating meat." I'm not a nutritionist; I can't tell anybody what to eat and what not to eat. She assumed I was going to tell her that because I avoid meat – it has to do with my personal appreciation of my body and my stomach.

But, what I refer to, is people who want to be well,

but decline to make changes in their lives. To begin with, this co-worker insists she is not willing to make a change she does not like, in order to eliminate something she does not like. In the end it is her body, therefore, her total decision.

We could philosophize about human behavior for many days and with many pages, but in the end I believe each one has their own philosophy of life.

What is good to mention is that we remember the teachers around us, never missing an opportunity to learn, moving forward and evolving our own philosophy about life.

Socrates said, "Philosophy is the search for the truth, as a measurement of what man must do and as a norm for his conduct." Well, it has been working for me, and for you? Did yours help you to find yourself?

If the answer is yes, in what condition or situation were you?

CHAPTER VIII

✹

THE ARRANGEMENTS

LET US SUPPOSE YOU'VE already found your own self – whether it cost you more or less time is not important. What really matters is what you think about that person you've just found. Right in front of you is the true you.

Right there is the person you always dreamed to be, not the one you are now. Are you going to retaliate … fight with yourself? Or even worse, are you going to feel pity because you are not even close to who you wanted to be and you feel you don't have time any more to make your dreams come true? This is the second part of the job. If you sit down to regret, there will not be changes, hence, or accomplishments.

"Development is the new man of peace." I like to

quote this phrase from Pope John Paul II, because although it seemed to be addressed to the nations, that is not necessarily the case. We are the ones who make the nations.

If you start working on your deteriorated self esteem, and start developing in the direction of your calling, you begin to feel peace – you are achieving something. Little by little, your mental and spiritual evolution climbs until you realize you are doing what you always wanted to do, and believe me, at times you don't even remember how it all started because you don't want to find your old personality inside of you.

I remember that in the beginning I listened to a cassette tape of a famous writer and spiritual lecturer. She explained all the changes she had had to make in her life to attain, first her spiritual goal, and then the cure of a cancer she had been diagnosed with. She gave a series of advice to help people in their process of change.

She cured herself, but was responsible enough to ask those listening to her tape, to alternate their method with traditional medicine. Out of what she said about herself, what really impressed me was that, when fighting to make her change -which as a matter of fact was funny -her first resolution was to stop talking about others.

She affirms – here comes the funny part – she spent weeks or months with her mouth closed, talking to nobody because she didn't have anything to say. One of the maladies humanity suffers is gossip. There are people that even act out the story and change their facial expressions when talking about others – trying to imitate them in a mocking way-to make the gossip more credible.

The truth is that more or less, gossiping is heard all around. The truth? Gossip is the first thing we must eliminate. If somebody has a defect so perceivable that others notice it, you don't have to go around like a cheap newspaper or magazine, touting it.

Part of the mechanics of the gossip is to expose others' defects, believing that in this way we look superior, but it's a lie.

The gossiper denigrates his or herself so much he or she generates two kinds of feelings – disgust or pity. I've always said and I uphold it – I never consume a product which says it's better than another brand. If you need to cheapen the other product to say yours is better, not even you can believe in it.

Superior things show themselves valuable with time. Likewise, trustworthy people spread their goodness and are their own recommendation. A lie can't be sustained for a whole life. And remember the proverb, "Tell me what you brag about…"

So, begin to work on yourself; live minute by minute; don't think about what might happen with your life in the future with the changes you've already attained and the ones you want to attain, because you are taking the risk of resting on accomplishments yet to be achieved. Do it at your pace, not mine; live and create your own experiences and not mine. These I mention strongly desiring that you know we can do it, but you have your interior chart and your own materials. Why should I worry about posterity? What has posterity done for me?

This was said by Groucho Marx, an American actor. He was right. Build a happy, healthy present. And that will be your posterity, the effect of that cause. Live here and now.

I always cite philosophers and famous characters who gave useful advice, before I did, or learned how to live before I did, because not only do I learn from the teachers in my daily life; but from those who have gone the way of Fame and Glory, and from those still alive who do it with the same dignity.

That is why I quote frequently. When I remember something I've read I like to cite it. On other occasions I look for a phrase in any book, which gives weight to my words.

A famous British novelist and dramaturge, Dame Daphne Du Maurier, once said, "At times this is how it happens in life:-- when it's the horses that have worked, it's the coachman who receives the tip."

This is what conniving is about, that the ones who have fought for an ideal before, or have developed a system which may be useful to others, reveal it. Somebody will always come along to make it better. The human race is in constant mental and spiritual development; hence, the old norms – no matter what they were at the time – have to be adapted to current life. We can't stay stuck in the past. Not even the speech of any language is the same anymore.

If my grandparents awakened from the dead with their old personality they'd have to relearn the language to understand me. At this moment, in order to realize a change in your life, you must ask and answer yourself in all honesty the following: "What do I think about me?"

You are probably saying to yourself the same thing most of my clients have told me, "I love myself very much," "I'm very proud," "I don't let anybody put me down," etc.

I can say with all assurance, that those who have accepted responsibility for what has happened to them up until now, are the ones who have made positive changes in life. Unfortunately, this is the minority. The rest, well, they continue with their problems and barriers, with their misunderstood pride, and para noia – thinking others want to put them down and their famous and misunderstood pride.

Once in my job, I remember I was conversing with a co-worker. At the other end of the room, a group laughed and murmured something which I didn't understand. My co-worker said to me, "I feel very bad, they're laughing at us." Without waiting for another comment I said, "You know? This morning when I looked at myself in the mirror I saw a happy woman with nothing that could provoke mocking."

Well, somehow those who were laughing got closer and one of them -by the way, there's always somebody who dares to show her face – said to me; "A while ago, we were laughing at you." As if I had been waiting for it, I immediately replied, "Really? Thanks for letting me know that I was able to provide you with a moment of gladness; it's good to know there are nice people who know how to laugh." She seemed disconcerted and added, "I was joking, how can you think I was laughing at you?" Her expression was different from the mocking one she had come with.

"If you want results, don't do the same thing all the time." Albert Einstein.

Dare to change. People love and look to imitate those who accept their own challenges and surrender themselves in pursuit of an improvement. And this must be because our commitment is with the Universe; we are a beautiful part of it.

Don't let inactivity take hold of you; exploit your human non-conformity to do something for yourself. Don't do as the fool or the coward who lays hold of the idea that others are worse. Use the daily teachers; don't forget it.

I read this proverb some time ago; I don't know where it came from or who the author is, but it's to the point: "I was furious for not having shoes; then I found a man with no feet, and I felt content with myself."

That is good for people who have decided to be conformist – and notice I don't say conformable – you must have conformity as part of patience, a beautiful virtue as you move from one transition to the other -but if you want shoes, even if you don't have feet, buy your shoes.

You have the right to possess all you want, as long as you don't drag others in your change and fulfillment of your desire. Everyone has the right to his or her own life and to have time of change. Remember, the person who doesn't want to change, has a vocabulary full of excuses for not doing it. Let the person scrutinize his or herself and become aware of what he or she needs in his or her own time. He says he's not a conformist and for years he or she repeats that, but deep inside he or she is. The proof is that it does the same, speaks the same, land like a parrot, repeats everything heard, through the years without changing a single thing, at times without having the knowledge of what he or she is saying.

These people normally either haven't done anything productive in life, or have accomplished everything and have lost it all because nobody could say anything or suggest to them what to do.

And yet, they don't bow down to their misplaced pride, and they deceive themselves that it's not the time to change, and they come to the age of enjoying what they did, but are still waiting for the moment to make a decision to change.

Believe me, this kind of person, we have to leave. Most of them die like that; they don't change and need more lives and blows to open their eyes. They like to dress well and have good meals, but they say money does not interest them to cover their lack of will. Well then, what do they buy their steaks with?

If money is not their priority, what are they doing, fighting in the jungle of materialism? There's no one blinder than the person who does not want to see. We have to leave them, so they can live from past glories and from their inadequate and outdated philosophy.

To this kind of person I'd answer with a phrase from Indira Gandhi that reads, "The world demands results. Do not tell others about your labor pains. Show them the baby." – a wise phrase.

But remember, true success isn't getting there, but knowing how to stay there, so don't show a photo of a baby who doesn't exist anymore, or tell the story of how good he was. To stay on target – although this is apparently in our hands – requires effort and continuous work, and I say, apparently in our hands, because you never reach your goal. Just when you think you are there, I assure you, your anxious spirit will take you farther. We are a product of The Source; hence, we'll never stop co-creating and recreating.

A Hindu proverb says, "There's no one tree the wind hasn't shaken, so we have to be strong in our decisions because the shaking will come."

WHAT IS PROSPERITY?

PROSPERITY IS THE FAVORABLE course things take. What people call good luck is also success in what is undertaken, happens or takes place.

Many people, whom I asked, agreed that prosperity is wealth; obviously some people do not conceive of prosperity without money.

From a spiritual point of view, prosperity begins inside of you; it is a state of richness--yes, but spiritual – which makes you feel capable of getting everything, because you are connected with the Providing Source. And of course, if you are really and honestly rich inside, wealth is going to show on the outside, according to the size you conceive it.

For many people, having it all, is having a little house or an apartment which can be afforded within their possibilities. For others, to have it all means properties, trips, automobiles, credit cards. Neither group is wrong. I say it again, you can wish and have all your mind is able to get, according to the extent of your dreams, but let nobody suffer on your way. Watch over your interior prosperity, because accordingly, the external will be given to you, one way or another.

There's the one who thinks there are bad people who have it all. The Universe neither makes a mistake, nor is unjust; somewhere in his evolutional career, he won what he's got now and also for some reason. He changed his manner later on—not keeping the work of love in his heart for some time. There is always the chance of losing all, or for disgrace to manifest itself.

The truth is none of us is free from going through a reckoning of one's life, so we must be ready or at least fortified, because I believe that in regard to serious pain, we aren't totally ready yet -at least, I am not.

I know there are civilizations where society is different from ours and they are prepared for suffering, in a different way. Others have suffered so much, they've hardened. But whatever our thinking may be, in my opinion, we must be prepared with a spiritual fortress.

All the rest comes later on. I got used to releasing my pain with music; that way, it diminishes until I can accept it. But it isn't easy at all. Thank God, it is not impossible, either.

Make a map of your prosperity. Some people use cardboard and glue images on it of the things they desire. They place it where they can see it most of the time to keep creating in their mind a view of what their future will be, and what their belongings will be.

You can use home magazines to decorate your map, as well as gluing the car of your dreams, a photo of a model which represents the personality of the mate you are looking for, in case you are single. Mind has no limit, neither the Universal gifts, so put it into practice.

But please, don't lie in front of your picture, waiting for all that you asked for to get manifested, because life doesn't work that way. The Creation took a lot of work; you also have to work to accomplish yours.

Another way to do it is a list where you write down, line by line, the things you desire. Read your list every day; this helps your mind keep an image of what you want. Mark with a cross what is getting accomplished, and if you want, add new things. Don't give up; it is a privilege we all have; just believe in yourself. There is no discrimination in the Universe and God doesn't have favorite children.

The Indian philosopher and writer, Tagore said, "The forest would be very sad if only birds that know how to sing sang." So make up your mind, design your prosperity style inside of you and then bring it into your life, but don't lose your spiritual perspective, because if you achieve it – which is most likely – you're going to need it so you can keep it.

In the entire planet, there are millions of people to whom you can offer your calling for service, whether your dreams are sewing, construction, poetry, architecture, carpentry, plumbing, writing, music, singing, dancing, etc.

We are prepared to fill the gap anywhere. Why don't we achieve it? Because of fear and lack of faith in ourselves, let us not be content with crumbs if we can eat the entire loaf. We just have to remember not to leave anyone hungry on our way. If you open your physical and spiritual eyes, if you listen with both your human and soul's ears, you'll see and hear how many people – your neighbors – are looking for you, because they need you.

Once, a friend of one of the many religions which I belonged to, looking for my spiritual identity, said to me, "It's bad that you don't like to ask for help; you always offer help; don't you realize that without intention, you are being arrogant? And at the same time you deny to others the gift of giving of themselves, as it corresponds to all of us."

Was she ever right! To say we give, but if we don't like others to give to us, is an arrogant act. It is beautiful to give and receive, to feel that energetic communion produced by both actions.

When you realize how beautiful it is to be really useful, you will notice the difference between what you do now and what you want to do. Just the fact of being ourselves makes us happy. I'm sure you don't hurt anybody by being the real you.

If there are patterns around you which, due to social, family or religious issues are considered unbreakable, it is they who made these rules and who insist on following them. It is they who hurt themselves; not he who decides to break them in search of his wings and his own wind, to fly over his life looking for his authentic freedom.

Remember, to defend your freedom doesn't mean to abandon your children, or expose them to a cruel life, so you can make yours. They will always be first; remember you are not just feeding little bodies, but you are preparing tomorrow's citizens. Whatever you program their minds with will be the future.

They mustn't be careless. If you act with your heart you'll realize they are not tying you down; they are the most important people in your life; they're the closest students you have, and the sweetest and most wonderful way to evolve – learning how to give with no conditions. Besides being your students, they are your best teacher because you learn from them, how to begin to be the best being on the planet, to edify your life, to forgive your shortcomings.

And with that kind of foundation, who could collapse that building? Always keep in mind my first

Metaphysics class. The teacher told us to begin exercising our patience, a difficult task in the fast life we live so full of accidents, but it is not impossible.

He mentioned those drivers who we share our streets and highways with, day by day. He said that if we try to see our loved ones in each culprit who crosses in front of us, those who cut in front of us, speeding just to pass, we could understand and begin to tolerate. And at the same time, we'd do a big favor to our heart, stomach and liver, by staying calm.

It's true, the first time I came across this, my reaction was to think, "This person thinks the street is his." I immediately recalled my professor's words and I thought of him as my daughter. My perspective changed totally. "Poor man, he must be tired and hungry after a hard day's work. Heavenly Father, Bless and protect him."

How easy it was to change my perception about that person. Why is it that if we can justify the mistakes of our loved ones, we can't do it with others? Because we aren't programmed to love others as we love our children, ourselves or anybody. Simply, some time we were taught we should love, that was a commandment. Orders in our life all the time – the ones with no basis – have never worked; they are not working and will not work.

Many years have gone by. I don't need to compare anybody with my daughters so that I can feel compassionate love.

If I hear an ambulance siren, if on my way I come across an accident on the highway, if the police is in pursuit or questioning somebody, I immediately say, "Thank you Universal Energy for your presence in this place, thank you because I know only Your Justice will manifest there. I declare health and life in whatever situation that occurs." I may say any other positive affirmation that comes to mind at that moment. This is just an example.

It's very likely that when I finish my affirmation I'm already far from that place, but I am sure that with the power conferred on me before birth, when I was still a spark in process of evolution, I mobilized the spiritual forces in the Major Kingdom that take care of this kind of circumstances.

I go totally confident that the law of cause and effect is also carried out in good works, and although I didn't do it thinking of myself at that moment, something in my being lets me know that I am also being protected by Love.

I don't want confusion to exist, because many people who are not prepared for the change or don't believe in what I present here, unfortunately use the words or actions of those who have tried to give a helping light against confusion.

This doesn't mean that the person who does this is exempt from having an accident; there are situations which are already given and meant to happen in our life. What unconditional love assures us is that the same treatment we gave, "at the time and in the time", in the moment we may need it will be returned to us.

God will never go bankrupt, because He always pays.

We know now that He doesn't punish. What we know as punishment is the consequence of what we did, when we determined our "trip" of freedom, to become "Beings of Light", with greater aspirations. To be prosperous and happy.

CHAPTER IX

✻

IF YOU SEE YOURSELF PORTRAYED IN THIS BOOK

IF YOU FEEL THAT what you have read is a photograph of your soul, or if in some of my comments you think I'm talking about you, that's right, but it is nothing personal.

I have only portrayed my inner life-which is akin to yours-and followed the changes in my soul step by step. What you do, I do; what you've done, I did, and what you will do, I also will do. There's nothing new under the sun-nor in us.

We are the perfect children of God. There is not a mistake more beautiful than ours; that's what we came for – to make mistakes so we can keep going, in order to go back home with pure energies.

Everything in The Creation has its opponent. How are we going to be good if we haven't been bad? How will we find out that we want to be a Light if we haven't walked in darkness? How will we know we don't want to be wrong if we haven't been wrong? How can we choose what we want to be if we have not been that? How to compare without knowledge? How can we know we want to see if we haven't been blind?

When we were a spark of the Great Sun-- which is The Creating Energy, Jehovah, God, Universe, Allah, or however you feel comfortable calling Him-- we used to receive it all; we had no more knowledge besides that given to us.

But we were and we are sparks from the Great Sun, and we wanted to blaze, so we asked for our right to do it. We didn't want to be useless receptors; we were and are potential gods, so we were given the freedom to exercise as givers, but child-like givers. Our growth is difficult but certain; sooner or later we will finish our career as little creators to become great universal co-creators. To do this we have to learn to overcome obstacles.

When you asked for your independence, this was delivered to you with all its contents. That is, with two sides to everything; you choose and you evolve.

The road is so long that we can not even stop to look forward. It is here and now where we want to think and work. We are building-remember that- no builder does tomorrow's work today; nor would he have done it yesterday. It sounds contradictory doesn't it?

We are creating now. Let us not stop – it is subtly delicious; it provides superhuman pleasure which is nice, as you will see.

LEARNING TO USE YOUR FREEDOM

MUCH HAS BEEN SAID about freedom through the years. However, we, the children of God and Man have demonstrated by our behavior that we know nothing about it.

Yes, it is true that freedom is the natural faculty a human being has to act one way or another- or do nothing- and he is responsible for his actions; but freedom also carries an important aspect – public responsibility. We can't go around the world hurting people and nature. Being inhuman and making international and internal wars for the sake of freedom, because the freedom you think you have to impose is the same that others have for not accepting it

This is why I admire and quote a great Mexican Patrician whom I try to emulate every day of my life. In all honesty, this brings me problems because our so-called freedom is not really known by many, and through our ignorance we arrive at one of the civic conditions we ignore the most, sometimes in the name of love, and what is worse, in God's Name.

Mr. Benito Jua'rez left us with a phrase which is profound, intellectual, ethical and, extremely simple so that it can be comprehended by anybody, and it is readily understood even by a child of school age. I quote: "The respect for others' rights, means peace."

Isn't that wonderful? How much happiness would be generated if each of us could exercise that right without hurting anybody? And I'm not talking about anarchy. Among all the things that I want to do and that I do in my life is to respect the current laws, whether just or unjust. The truth is, you have the same freedom to join the system which suits you, according to your criteria, but wherever you are, respect the law – there are no rights without obligations.

After briefly going over what freedom is, we go on to see what you do with your freedom and how you use it.

Remember this is about making changes, which will make your life full of happiness. This can't happen if you have trampled on somebody in order to achieve it. Even though it is true that nobody should interfere in your life on a whim, it is also true that the freedom I'm talking about involves making favorable changes to your life, which in turn generates spiritual and mental health, and as a result, your physical health.

This can't hurt anybody. On the contrary, it is going to rebound in benefits for people around us. I want to make this clear because there are still people to whom you talk about yoga or meditating and they say you are going to hell, and that is not Christian, or favorably viewed by God.

To defend your position at that moment, with love, with no offense or discussion is right, and you are giving an example of peace. You can't stop your spiritual progress because somebody, who may be close to you, thinks differently. As in everything in life, time will demonstrate who is wrong. The Teacher said, "Wherefore by their fruits ye shall know them." If the results of your acts are positive, who will accuse you of doing something wrong?

Consciously program what you desire for your life. You can conceive all you want – your mind is the only thing, until now, which can bring about great thing; it has no limit and it is the best instrument you have within your reach.

I can just suggest ideas about this. The only person who knows what your heart desires is you-perhaps you wish to begin studying, to continue or practice that career you left behind. In contrast, you may want to rest from your working life and build something new in your family with some foundation more solid than money. Your dream may be a house, a car, to marry the ideal person, to improve your physical, mental, spiritual health, etc.

Our scope of dreams is vast and can include one or all of the things already mentioned, but whatever your choice might be, get to work on it with the assurance that it is yours, that you have achieved it even before this manifests.

Meditation is important because it helps you center yourself and place your life in a divine order. It is easier to live when you meditate; little by little, you see that without realizing it your life is changing. Use meditation to visualize your life in the way you want it; try to make your visualization so real that it is manifested in a way you truly believe is real life. Many of the things you desire can already be in a natural order in your way and the creative visualization will make it happen sooner in your life.

Remember that all your mind conceives is simply a reminder of something you know was already given to you. As you start practicing your visualization, you will begin realizing how everything will be provided to you according to your desires. This will also be, in accordance with what should come into your life, depending on your effort for your evolution.

I think I don't have to remind you that faith plays a very important role in this. If you don't believe in yourself, don't wish for it because it will not come – nor do I want you to believe in me – I just ask you to try. I'm sure you'll be amazed by your attainments, and even more, you will love them.

THE JOY FROM ATTAINMENTS

SLOWLY, YOU'LL START NOTICING favorable changes in your environment – people you thought were disagreeable begin to look amazing to you or at least agreeable. When you go shopping it is easier to find a place to park – which is now next to the store you want to visit – and even the traffic lights wear their "nice green suit" to give you a welcome to the intersection, inviting you to cross without danger.

These are just some of the small achievements at the beginning of your change. Even though they are small, they reassure you that you are on the right path, and that is the reassurance you need to get the rest.

Many people fall on their way because they listen to others. There are those whose empty lives are lived without direction and who are always placing little obstacles on the way and tell you it is pure coincidence, but believe me, coincidences do not exist, just causality.

Among all the many things I've read, I remember a very nice philosophical thought by an author whose name and book title I can't remember. I quote: "People are made out of the same substance as dreams." So then, let's use our own authentic raw material to produce a better life for ourselves; as a consequence, a better world will exist for those following.

Just think about those words mentioned above which remind us we were God's dream. That's why we were made out of His raw material, which had the same substance of His dream which makes us, as I've said, potential gods. Let's manifest ours as well, and let's be happy with each little or big accomplishment, and receive each change with the same happiness that The Creator manifested each time he materialized some wish. Likewise, it is very important to conti nue growing in our achievements.

TEACHING YOU TO BE HAPPY

A GREAT DEAL OF your achievements, besides a great amount of faith in yourself, is to be happy. I think the word happiness confuses people – if you show happiness to people, either they fear or criticize you.

Many people think that it is practically impossible to be happy in this life full of negative circumstances, diseases, and problems, sometimes affecting even our loved ones, and that he who says or appears to be happy, is lying.

While it is true that when we go through a difficult time, happiness lessens and faith momentarily weakens, it is also true that he who has spiritual training is able to work through the situation without the desperation which characterizes a person who suffers spiritual poverty.

There is a big difference between the person who knows there's a solution for his situation and the person who sits down to cry and to recite his liturgical prayer, asking for mercy.

If the circumstance changes, which is more likely, the person has nothing to recover from since he is not physically and emotionally devastated. On the contrary, he has taken a big step in his spiritual growth, which combined with the one he already had taken, make him a stronger person than before.

Having reached a higher evolutionary stage, his faith of course has also grown. We ask ourselves, what else is there in his life of plenty? If you guessed, there is more happiness than before the challenge.

However, there is another situation, and if the circumstance wouldn't disappear, should he, for a matter of karma, avoid that situation? His pain would be less and his recovery and acceptance would be quicker.

Unlike the help we seek from others, the help we give ourselves is much more secure and private, and except if you want to share your experience later to help others, nobody has to find out about your private experiences.

I believe in professional therapeutic help, if you don't feel capable to begin your change by yourself, look for a professional therapist. Never trust a friend or a person you know with your spiritual health. Despite their good intentions, perhaps their advice will be based on personal experience, which they may still be bitter about and the advice might not be what you need.

I think that before accepting advice from somebody, look at the fruits of their actions; if the person does not emit light which shows happiness, that person is not equipped to help others. I remind you, as I mentioned before, be cautious with the falsely happy person – there are many ways to identify him or her.

PROJECTING YOUR HAPPINESS

ONE OF THE THINGS that will help you more, and others, is the projection of your happiness. This is very important, just as in the same way you want other people to project their happiness to you, therefore you must project it.

Many times, in the bliss produced by happiness, we forget there are people around us who suffer. I can't ask you to hide your happiness because I don't hide mine, but you must look around us because many times, we have beside us people going through difficult times and they don't understand or believe in happiness because they haven't evolved to that point.

These people could get angry with us and become envious which means that we, unconsciously, are a stumbling block for them. Instead of helping them, we plunge them lower into that negative energy from which we sometimes wanted to get out, to emerge into the light that now we care for so fervently.

When we have people around us who talk only about problems, who always criticize others and you notice it is hard for them to see good qualities in their neighbor, we must work it out with care. Remember we have to pass on what we've received, but not everybody is ready to receive it, in fact, there are people who may decline to change.

The best way is to help; there's always something we can do for somebody. We must also give love, much love without limit. Remember love is the only thing that grows as much as we give, it does not end; normally, people are rebellious because they lack love and the companionship they want; it doesn't matter if they aren't alone, they feel they are, and they don't have spiritual richness to fill this emptiness.

Everybody likes to be loved, even those who deny it, therefore, a good way to show your happiness is by giving love to these people. They will feel so good that soon they'll start making changes in their life – perhaps they do not notice it, but you will.

We can't pretend their change will happen the next day, yours was not and nor was mine. In fact, the change goes with you in all of your earthly lives, there will always be something to surpass and at some point you will fall and will have to stand up again; the important thing is to get rid of the dust and continue walking.

That is one way – it has worked for me and I am sure it'll work for you as well. Keep in mind that your greatest challenge is to help the one who hurts you, the one who ignores you, the one who slanders you, and why not, the one you dislike. But don't confuse love and humility with a lack of respect; your self esteem is above all this. If you don't love yourself, you do not have love to give, the line is very fine and easy to cross, but as you keep moving forward, it will be easier to see it.

There are people we have to forgive and let go – not another thing can be done. At least I haven't been able to do it within the stage of evolution which I've reached. I haven't found a solution to understand some people who, although they have it all, don't have a thing. With all their knowledge, they still don't make changes.

CHAPTER X

�֍

CRITICISM BY OTHERS

I HAD THE QUALITY, and I think it is a great quality, of not caring for the opinion of others as far as destructive criticism is concerned. Many years ago I learned that people who feel the need to talk badly about others have a serious problem of self-esteem and confused identity. I believe all those who are certain about their capabilities and limitations, who know they can fail anytime, don't go around criticizing everybody else.

I emphasize this because if you have never been criticized, you will be, when you begin to change.

While it is true many people marvel at your change and it is also true you will attract beautiful, evolved people to your life with a fragrant soul, it is not less true that you will also find on your way, some who come close to you to tell you negative things. Some even say we are crazy, but who knows the difference between craziness and sanity?

The best attitude in this circumstance is to take things with love. That will be one of your challenges to develop unconditional love, because he who rebels against a change is not prepared even himself, and you can not require anybody to believe what you believe, but be comforted knowing that Joan of Arc was considered crazy, and many scientists, writers, musicians, and people in all kinds of professions, religious and social were called crazy in their time. You'd be amazed to find out who they were.

So, don't worry and keep going, this is a path we have to walk with conviction. We mustn't allow any doubt each time this comes, because it will come and it'll come many times – cast it out and say to yourself: I am on the right path for me, because this is what I want to do and I have all the permission and support from the universe to do it.

Once you have decided your change is for real, and nothing and nobody will stop you, begin designing your lifestyle – the one you'd like to have, how you want to live, what you want to do in the area of work. Consider trying to find out your true calling, because where your calling is your talent is as well. What matters is that, during this process, you have so much enthusiasm that you enjoy it and feel happy.

Have you ever been on a diet? Well, that is the enthusiasm I expect from you; when we are on diet, we are happy preparing the project, we look at the scale everyday, do exercise, we try new recipes; some of us visit nutrition centers, gyms, etc.

This is exactly the same. After all, when you begin to improve your spiritual body, you are removing pounds of wrong actions from your conscience – you're going to start downloading your energetic body and you will feed your mind with new recipes of positivism and love.

You can even do meditation exercises to keep you peaceful and calm and to gain the necessary preparation to go out in the world and be able to manifest love, no matter how the day unfolds.

We also have 'gyms' in this area. If you are one of those who need help, or it seems difficult for you to do it, there are just hundreds of centers everywhere – there, you can meditate in a group. The energy generated in a group meditation is wonderful, after all, there are people in that place who are concentrated in love and healing energy and this fills the place, and your body is also being cleansed and healed at that moment.

You may attend Reiki circles, Kabbalah schools, or Yoga; indeed there's much help for all of those who want it; these reunions are free, as well as the Kabbalah. Truth does not have any charges, try it, look, all you do for your change which doesn't hurt anybody is perfect.

RECYCLE, IT IS FASHIONABLE

I DON'T SAY THIS with irony, I recycle out of conviction. I feel we owe the planet the responsibility to
recycle to see if this way there will be less deforesta-
tion and we can keep the integrity of our beloved Gaia
intact, our beautiful and long suffering planet, which
in the end, is our mother as well.

Of course I'm talking about your life at this moment, but it is a good thing that you know a great help
for your change is to begin making a small effort in
the care of the environment. This is a beautiful way
to start the change, as well as respecting all kind of
lives, including those which may seem less important
for you, for example, a cockroach's.

But, we'll talk about this later, now we are going to
see how to recycle your life. We must learn to educate
ourselves.

There are things we want to leave behind, that we
consider to be our waste and yet these are recyclable.
This is the best foundation to build on because we
are a Divine Seed; so even the wastes of our useless
existence will bring life to a new and healthy person
in the same manner the tree's leaves when they fall
and fertilize the ground where the fruit will fall and
will produce new life.

A friend of mine sent me a profound thought which
I'd like to share with you because we never think it
can happen until somebody reveals it to us. It says,

"Half of the work done in this world is to make

things appear what they are not" Elias Root Beadle.

Isn't it a pity that this really happens around us? After receiving this message, I made a little effort to find out where this opinion comes from.

Notice that many people do things they don't really want to do to pretend something. Some of them you observe don't even do things right – they just make them appear as if they are well done. A short time ago, I received this message, so there was not enough time to elaborate on an observation of what I mention here, but the truth is, that maybe one of the reasons why things are not functioning at their optimum on the planet, is because even though they appear to be made, when we need them they don't work because they just *appeared* to be made.

And with this, I mean everything; there are a whole lot of things which don't work, and yet, in some people's eyes, everything looks fine.

A few days ago, a man who lives, well, if one can live on a pension, told me he asked for some help from the government in order to receive help with food. After doing all the necessary calculations, an employee sent him a letter telling him, that because he had two hundred dollars left every month, they could only approve ten dollars per month for him.

My name must be Alice in Wonderland and without realizing it, I have come to a country of wonders because if one can eat on ten dollars a month, then I've died and gone to Heaven and I hadn't noticed.

According to what this man tells me, the two hundred dollars that is left is after he pays his mortgage, but he's got some other expenses such as the electrical bills, cleaning items, and personal hygiene. He must have enough even to have fun one day a month if he wanted to; this is more than just human necessity, it is a matter of common sense.

Well then, I believe right now that Mr. Elias Root Beadle's thought fits exactly; this is a rule or a law that is made to appear as if it functions. I hope this book falls into the hands of those who have the power to revise and understand what is being done with some laws, those who have been entrusted with their execution and feel they have the power to approve or veto a petition. In this case, as I witness, the petition was made by somebody who had never asked for a thing from anybody, and had worked very hard all of his life.

If we were energetically connected as we should be, I am sure all laws would work better. I don't think the agent who attended this man should break the rules, I think laws must be respected to create order, but I also believe that if they use a little love and good will, things can be improved. Each rule or law is full of formalities to which an agent can adhere, in order to provide the maximum service to a citizen so he is, if not completely satisfied, at least not humiliated.

It is not just an opinion of mine; in reality, the lack of love has become some kind of social-spiritual cancer, which is taking us to such a level that if we don't pay attention soon, what our children will inherit is an uninhabitable world.

My boss told me: If the whole world knows what you are talking about, what are people waiting for to change?

We are all students and teachers; let us then practice our capacity to love. If you have any doubt in being able to do it, take your time at this moment, please close this book and see where your loved ones are, look at them, feel them, what do you wish for them? They are your elders, your children, your grandchildren, your brothers.

Do you now dare to try the change and begin to see them be truly happy? The choice is yours, only you can decide the change and I know it is difficult. It is as if we had to turn ourselves inside out like a dress, but you'll gain so much, that I'm going to suggest you try it only as a test to see if it works for you because I know at the end you'll get a lot. Don't let what you're reading go to waste; there's no worse battle than that which is not attempted, and the worst decision in your life was the one you didn't make, so simply dare to do it!

STRIVING FOR ACCOMPLISHMENTS FOR YOU AND OTHERS

YOU'VE ALREADY REALIZED THAT, not only in math class, one plus one equal two. Numerology is implicit in all our existence, so, all we do results in damage to us, you, me and to our neighbor. We all affect the planet and destabilize the universal energy if we act irresponsibly. The responsibility we have is so big; isn't it best to begin to assume it? After all, we are here because we asked so then let's do it right.

This is the way it works: when you think you hurt yourself only that is not true. You are not a solitary cell in the universe of "who knows," you are here with me, with the rest; you are working in our favor or against us. You are an inhabitant of this Universe, the world that came to existence because of a shared Divine Desire, and in which you are a wonderful resident with gifts and powers you can't even imagine at this moment.

When somebody besides you coughs, you move away and you even worry or get upset because that person did not cover his mouth. Now, I ask myself, do you worry in the same way when you have an outburst of rage and pollute the environment with negative energy? This is also contagious, or what is worse, do you get irritated and angry when exercising your right to smoke in public, you irresponsibly force others to be passive smokers? Haven't you read that cancer is a murderer worse than a cold?

Then, think it over, because we are quick to defend ourselves, we must also be quick to defend others. Learn to exercise your rights correctly if these are harmful, it doesn't matter whether it is legal; they are not being used in the correct manner.

There is a wonderful sentiment human beings experience when we give. That is why TV marathons to collect funds are so popular and successful. People in general like to feel good; it is very strange that somebody feels proud of being bad. Yes, there are some, but I don't believe them. That is a seed somebody planted in their minds. Years ago it germinated, it wasn't uprooted in time; the person has such low self esteem, that he or she prefers to say that they are bad to defend his or herself from an environment which he or she thinks will reject.

The truth is we must keep that loving attitude of unconditional love all year around, not only when there is a TV marathon, a natural disaster or a serious accident. We must give all year, as much as we can. If a million people could agree to send a dollar each to hospitals for kids with cancer, AIDS or to any other institution or to combat disease, we'd be talking of one million dollars every month, which is really needed to cover the expenses of their treatments. Haven't you ever seen a mother asking for help so her son or daughter can have surgery?

All of us together can make a difference, and this would be the change which would save humanity.

Then, I ask myself now, would it be easy for a million people to agree, when in a family of only three or four, there is chaos?

Among all of us, I repeat, we can do it. It is not easy, but thank God it is not impossible.

There are ways to help, which have nothing to do with money. We have people around us with a great lack of spirituality and I am not talking about religion, many of these people are attending churches and apparently believe and practice their teachings, but they live in sad homes where fights take place everyday. The children are not responsive and the environment is a real disaster.

We could start inviting these people to the places we've begun visiting, talking to them and letting them know that life is something more than an Armageddon, that our world contains beauty, hope, achievements, and self-esteem.

Recommend a good book that has helped you in your first steps. For example, I always recommend the first book of metaphysics, which I read. I still keep it on my night table and I review it now and then, this is why I recommend it at the end of reading this book.

Try to find out the person's motivations. Some human beings are moved by what 'others will say', some by family morals, others by their religion; try to make them understand all of that is good as long as it makes them happy and produces fruits in their familiar, social and professional environment. If not, changes have to be made, cut a little here, add a little there; you never want to go against their old-fashioned and well established ideas because you can create a block and a lot of confusion. Just plant your seed with no effort, in a placid, loving manner and let the seed germinate. Help anytime you can and be an example of power, when a small-minded person meets somebody whose goals and efforts break the barriers of the word "impossible," he becomes self-motivated, believe me it is true. I am a product of it, and yes, I am an earthling just like you.

Remember each personal achievement is a gift to others. When you improve, you are a better person for your neighbor, therefore, you are teaching something of value. Never forget your position of universal teacher, show all the beauty because when you do it, you are attaining something.

You have no idea what a smile can do in the mind of a discouraged or irritable person. A few months ago, some parents came to the center where I worked in the childcare area. They brought a girl who visited us for the first time, but despite the colorful place, the kids playing and having fun, the girl didn't feel good and cried because she was left there.

No matter what she was shown or told, the girl was very reluctant to stay. I watched, from the other side of the room, the parents' effort to leave the girl there and the girl's determination to defend her right to say no.

I didn't want to intervene because there was a co-worker trying to welcome the little girl, so I waited for a while and then I got close. After talking to the girl for a moment, she took my hand and decided to stay. I remember I told her parents, you see we convinced her, and her father told me, no, it was your smile that convinced her.

I felt good for the girl, the parents and for myself, and I rested assured the rest of the day – they felt the same.

For this reason, think all the time about a smile and put it on your face before leaving your house. You are teaching somebody else that a smile has light, is positive, cures sadness, changes a bad mood, and what else – it is contagious.

I am sure to have covered in general what I meant to tell you. All that is here can be proved easily; changes are difficult especially if they are radical, but it is not impossible to bring them about. Those who came before me taught me the way. Now I teach you; conduct your experiment; I am sure you'll like it, but what you will like more, is the total success which follows the change. There's a saying I once heard, "I am not a gold coin so that everybody can like me." You know what, after you change, most people will like you, even though that coin is not in your own pocket.

The right portion on each occasion will be a good start; each of us knows his own extent of his capabilities. Don't force yourself to learn, or to teach because you may quit at the beginning or at the middle of the path – this is long and it continues for all of your existence, in each step you carry out this plan.

THE MEDITATION

MANY PEOPLE THINK MEDITATING is something difficult and that only people who are highly trained can do it. There are people who have even asked me if they need to study or belong to a certain group in order to meditate.

Nothing is farther from the truth; meditation is for everybody – no need to study. If I were to tell you that most people meditate *regularly*, it may seem strange to you. The truth is that every time we fall into a state where we move away from the reality surrounding us, even for a moment, so that we can concentrate on something bothering us, or that we feel is a problem, we are meditating. It is not the right way to do it because when you concentrate on a negative situation, instead of disappearing, it increases and becomes something more serious. We should never feed negative circumstances by thinking or talking about them. If we use this same technique and we adapt it to positive thoughts, we are beginning to recreate the life for which we were created.

You do not have to fail to grasp the point in order to meditate. In fact, I believe, and this is a very personal opinion, that if you are trying to be creative there must be something beautiful in your mind. I have heard many comments from people who have approached me to ask how they can do that. Yes, you can do it, but I do not think it is easy to start right there.

There are many meditation methods; I have participated in several techniques and then I have practiced this method with my clients which I am explaining to you. Even for myself, having a little more training than a beginner, it is easier to do it this way. I have made it so much a part of my life to the point that I can do it in public, and the noise does not bother me, and this is something I want to talk about.

If you get used to getting in touch with The Light, your 'Superior I', in a place with a profound silence, what will you do when you face a difficult situation? Either, you will not know what to do, or you are going to get violent, which will make you lose your grip in a situation you had handled before hand.

I meditate everyday, but I like to take my little escapes when there are people around me as well, of course not when I am working, or on duty in something that demands my concentration. I have practiced in shopping centers because crowds amaze me. I easily receive a lot of energy from people, and that facility to escape makes me feel very good; it helps me cleanse myself from those energies in a matter of a few minutes.

So it does not matter what meditation method you use. I have noticed no variation in the results. You just have to concentrate in order to create them.

It is very similar to creative visualization. I'd say it is the same because you are creating and if you want to create peace, you can do that by auto programming yourself. You do not have to let your mind go blank in order to do it, nor do you need another person to guide you either, unless you are like me in the beginning when I always had to attend group meditation meetings. This was due to the need for encouragement coming from those who got into this discipline before I did and from those who were looking for a way to change their life, just like I did.

That energy generated in a room of people meditating is unique. I think, for you, it would be good to look for meditation groups and Reiki circles, in case you are not a regular visitor, where you can gather and learn by practicing what you are reading here, and experiment with that energy of light, which gives peace and, above all, security in a world where everybody is constantly talking about insecurity.

Meditation is always helpful in all circumstances. In a meditative state you can find answers to a number of questions you have had during your whole life, as well as those that are fresh in your memory now. It is also good to find solutions – you get to know your inner being and you learn who you really are and the potential you have. You overcome fears and develop the capability to do many things you had dreamed about, but unconsciously you were denying yourself. Saint Thomas of Aquinas said, "There is nothing in the intellect that has not been in the senses first." This is how all that exists was created in the universe; everything was in the Sense of the Creating Energy – it then became a desire and this was manifested.

So begin to wish for something; make your meditation a wonderful assistant to create beautiful things in your environment. I know a person who demonstrated this to me, that as soon as she began to change her thoughts from negative to positive, her life began to become full of light.

She tells me she changed the music she listened to for classical music and when she felt like listening to a song she would listen to those with a positive message.

Songs that did not talk about failures or the desire to die for somebody. She told me she blames herself for the failure in her emotional life, for trying to emulate those long suffering heroines in novels who would always be a winner at the end, staying with the man who annoyed, mistreated, humiliated and abandoned them.

After listening to this I think I felt a little identified with her and perhaps, many readers feel the same. This woman stopped listening to the news which filled her with panic; therefore, she no longer scared her children with advice full of fear, more than just simple precaution. The truth of the matter is I never mentioned this to her, but this is one of the methods I use in my own life. The good woman of our story told me that her life has made a three hundred and sixty degree turn around. There is greater happiness at home and both her husband and children feel better in her company. Of course, she now has beautiful things to talk about.

CHAPTER XI

THE GOOD ONES, THE ASPIRANTS AND THE IGNORANT ONES

MUCH IS BEING SAID about goodness and wickedness; as everything in creation, they are the extremes of one and the same energy, one could not exist without the other. How could anything be good if it does not have a point of comparison?

I heard somewhere, or perhaps I read it in a book, that a Catholic priest decided to join the army before the seminary; when his superiors asked him why he was doing this and if he was sure of his calling, he replied, "I am sure of what I want, but how am I going to fight evil if I do not know it?"

In my opinion, humanity is divided into three groups; the good ones, those who are working day to day to become that, and those who have not realized what they can become. This does not mean that evil does not exist; as I mentioned before, everything in the universe has its opposite. Those inflicted by evil are those people have not realized they can be good. Somebody has to do the work so that equilibrium exists. There would not be light without the union of a positive and a negative pole. I reveal to you the seven universal rules, according to Hermes Trimegisto:

1.- THE ALL is mind; the universe is mental.

2.- As it is up, it is down, as it is down it is up.

3.- Nothing is immobile, everything moves; everything vibrates.

4.- Everything is double, it has two poles; everything has its opposite: the similar and the opposite are the same; the opposites are identical in nature, but different in degree; the extremes touch each other; all the truths are half truths, every paradox can be reconciled.

5.- Everything flows and flows again; everything has its periods of advancement and regression, everything ascends and descends; everything moves as a pendulum; the distance to the right is the same as its movement to the left; the rhythm is the compensation.

6.- Every cause has its effect, every effect has its cause; everything happens according to the law, luck is nothing but the name given to an unknown law; there are many planes of causality, but nothing escapes from the law.

7.- Generation exists everywhere; everything has its masculine or feminine principle; generation manifests on all planes.

Therefore, we cannot judge those whom we consider bad or, as I say, they have not realized they can be good. How could you evolve if you had nothing to overcome? This is why I say it is a daily fight and a constant knowledge of ourselves in order to achieve it. The battle can be as easy or as difficult as you want; we have to learn to accept with love – that is what makes the battle easier.

OVERCOMING RESENTMENT

RESENTMENT IS ONE OF the biggest crimes in our society. That inflated ego that makes a human being say "nobody offends me and gets away with it," has damaged the world more ever since it was recorded, more than cancer or AIDS. However, it seems like people do not realize that a second of wrath can hurt many lives in no time at all.

Because we don't need anybody to know we were humiliated or mistreated verbally or physically, what makes a human being to be so dependent on his neighbor's opinion? It all begins at home. I do remember that in my home it was very important what people said and important not to bad mouth the family. For both my mother and father it was a cultural matter to have a good opinion about the family in our neighborhood and in our social milieu.

From the time we were very small we were taught to be subject to the neighbor's opinion. Watch a child when he falls; the first thing he does is to look around to find out whether someone saw him. If he finds someone looking at him what does he do? He cries, shame takes over; he feels humiliated because he has been told so many times that if he runs or jumps he might fall, that the message he receives about falling is bad. Therefore, everybody else will see he has failed.

In the center where I worked everyday, many children take a tumble. I used to observe them before getting close to them to see if it was a dangerous fall.

It has never happened, but we have to do it, it is the rule. I used to do this without being noticed, because they immediately tried to find out who saw them fall down, and as they realize that nobody was watching, what do you think they did? They just shake themselves off and continue doing the same thing that made them fall – they will keep doing it until they can do it without falling.

It is at that early age when we must put an end to the comments that could create some hang up or attitude in the future. Once, a colleague asked a boy to stop crying because she had a headache; she did not do it with a bad intention, but trying to get the boy to feel pity and be quiet.

The message? Totally wrong – children should not be told about illness and, much less should not be taught they can be blackmailed with it. The stronger and healthier a child sees you, they will have. The more confidence in you and in themselves. So we are going to improve the quality of the human beings who are in our care, the children, because adults have their own responsibility for themselves.

But we are going to talk about adults who went through all of that programming and today, they face insecurities which make them drink alcohol, smoke in excess, use drugs or be drug-dependent, overeat, and drink coffee all day long. Of course this picture I present is that of an adult with some type of emotional mal-adjustment and can go from a depression to a violent state with the least provocation.

Like all the changes we have to make during our lives, this is not easy and it is not fun either. When we have an ideal in our hearts and we do the same as when we start a diet, have a positive mind and program the change for the day, it can be done and it is much easier.

Alcoholics are taught to stay sober for twenty four hours only; this helps them to overcome the anxiety of the thought that they will not drink anymore in their lives. They feel completely capable of meeting that daily challenge and, thank God, most of them are accomplishing that. We can do the same with our anger. When leaving our homes, we program ourselves just for the day and we can think the same as when we are driving a vehicle, as I explained before.

We are going to think that each person around us is our son, father, mother, brothers, grandchildren, our mate, etc., the person whom we love the most. We say that, just for today, we will be kind, obliging, loving, understanding, and educated. I am not going to criticize anybody nor will I feel better than others. When somebody does anything against me which is not nice, I'll excuse that person as if he or she were somebody I love very much. I will think that perhaps the person is not a very educated person, but it was not his or her intention, or I will think he had a bad day and was not able to control his or herself.

Likewise, it may be you who are the victim of the same person everyday, and with your educated, classical attitude full of love you make a change in this person. For years, I have seen how people sometimes want to imitate, intentionally or unconsciously, a person who is doing something good or is unique at something.

You see the changes and you even think he or she looks like me more and more every day. It has happened to me for years and it does not bother me that people imitate my good actions because I do the same with others. I copy all of that which exalts me and helps me to be better. This is called mutual teaching and it is how this wonderful creation moves forward.

If you try to make a new change in your life everyday, you will see that very soon you will begin to feel like a better person. Of course, there are traits in our personality that have been ingrained in us for years. These are the most difficult to overcome; we must be honest with ourselves and see what part of our personality hurts our neighbor. We must become conscious about where we must start to work in ourselves. When I say honest I mean we must be careful.

If you are one of those who believe that you are good, keep looking until you find. The good people are not a large group found everywhere. They are very special beings who have been sent with a mission, just like Mother Theresa. The rest of the people are part of the other two groups. Those trying to improve or those who are not good and do not wish to improve.

Do a good search until you find a wrong part of your personality you have or you want to change first, but always take a good look inside your heart and your memory. Begin to look for those things you remember with pain or anger; it is that small or big bitterness which you must remove. Afterwards, I promise, the rest is much easier.

In case you think you have no bitterness towards anybody, listen to yourself when you talk about somebody whom you don't like or why not think about somebody who hurt you or told you something that hurt you. Try to decipher what you really think about that person when you remember him; what do you feel against that neighbor? Anger? That is bitterness.

Pity? Why? Don't you think pity makes us a superior being? Do not confuse compassionate love with pity; one is a divine feeling that impels us to help; the other is a miserable feeling given to humiliate someone.

A customer told me that she has not given way to a bitter feeling for anybody in all of her life, but every time she can, she makes negative comments about her mother for some past behavior.

On one occasion another customer appeared to completely *ignore* her own anger or resentment, and that she could not even feel that towards anybody. We talked for more than one hour and she told me in detail how badly her husband had treated her, and how she even remembers day to day the humiliations he put her through, but yet she says she has forgiven him many years ago. Can you understand it? I don't either.

In her euphoria and emotional urge to vent her feelings she told me about another person from her family – how could he have been so ungrateful that he paid her back badly, for all the help she had given him when he needed it and later, she told me as she cried she had even kept a distance from her own brother because of a misunderstanding which was never clarified.

I tried to make her understand, that in all her conversation, she had poured out bitterness and bad memories about people she once loved, and that I was sure she still loved. But she did not give herself an opportunity to acknowledge it, to try to see pure energy within each of the human beings she had talked about, the same indivisible energy she had. Therefore, she was hating and judging herself. She did not understand it, nor did she want to, nor was it the time to do so.

The truth is she told me I was wrong and she'd rather not talk about it anymore. She got away from me, but I've been told by mutual friends she is attending group therapy and that she has changed so much and that her life has improved considerably. This is what matters, not that she did not do it when I talked to her, but when she accepted deep in her heart, her mistake, and deflated her inflated ego.

We have to adjust the way we weigh our resentment and bitterness and forgiveness. Let us try to turn cordiality, which is only a product of social education, into unconditional love which is produced by God.

I am sure this is how we can evolve and collaborate so that everything around us improves. There's no doubt in my mind that this is the example we wish to give to our children and we know it is the most important inheritance we can leave for them.

In my center where I worked, a conversation between two people took place; both were proud of having done the impossible to disappear from their ex-husbands because they had suffered too much with them and I asked myself, are the husbands the ones suffering more from this separation? No, their children are the ones suffering. These mothers, unintentionally, have planted a subliminal message in their minds that perhaps, although they didn't realize that they had been neglected by their fathers – that one of the most important beings in their life did not love them. Therefore, the mothers have planted contempt and doubt in their hearts.

These are the crimes society does not punish, but when the time comes, life makes you pay. "There's no term without due date or unpaid debt either."

One day, a situation came up where I was able to prove there's not only bitterness in our hearts for something done to us. A person I know told me she did not want to immigrate to the United States and her mother did not want her to either, because an equal social state exists, and that is not true, that we all are not the same. In her country, she was a person of high class. This brought me to another reality, social bitterness.

Which social class are we talking about? The good class, the class of us who wants to be good, or the class that has not realized they can become good?

The true social class is in our hearts, a person with class would never make a comment which could minimize anybody socially, but on the contrary, they are kind, affable and educated. Love is the only thing that makes us human beings, special, and good people.

So let us remove bitterness from our hearts, bitterness that undermines our happiness and our progress because everything gets stuck in our lives when the energy from the light is obstructed by a miserable feeling. Let us allow this energy to flow and enjoy our change.

WHERE IS LAUGHTER?

AT TIMES I GET lost in my thoughts and I ask myself hundreds of questions; I think about something funny or a comment I made, or perhaps something foolish I said which makes me smile. Many times I burst into laughter.

Then I ask myself, where is laughter? When did people forget to smile?

I remember when the image of a little smiling face began to be popular. I do not know where it came from. Some say it exists in a rock on Mars, but at least I don't know whether that is true. I saw a picture of that rock years ago, but nothing indicates to me it was taken on Mars.

Who created it? Does it really have its origin in other world or spheres outside ours? Who knows – everything is possible. The universe is infinite and everything is energy. Therefore, everything is mind and all is life. The truth is I've never seen the signature of the one who created it; it was given for all humanity to use it, at least here on *Gaia*, our beloved planet, and I am sure it has been a gift of love.

I would love to know who created it, at least by that I make my wish public. It does not matter which dimension it belongs to, if it makes us smile, he is a being that is evolved.

Perhaps many people want to know the same as I do. What happens is that sometimes there are anonymous givers who follow strictly the maxim of the Teacher:

"let not thy left hand know what thy right hand doeth", but anyway, let us wait, the invitation is on.

If somebody wants to join this petition and contact me, just in case I receive an answer, at the end of this book you will find my address. You can, if you want, write me for any reason. I am here for you.

Some time ago I made some cards in my computer – the kind one uses for business cards. These said: "smile, you have a pretty smile," and I left them with people who were a little rude or unpleasant in their dealings when I bought something or in some office where I was trying to get some information I needed.

Far from what I expected, everything turned out to be better from what I imagined. Nobody ever insulted me for that and, even some times, they thanked me and excused themselves, saying they were having a bad day or that something was wrong in their lives.

People respond. Not all who look disagreeable are that way. Look for His energy; contact Him mentally. If you are in the process of an honest change, this will work; on the contrary, you will get the answer from your own energy coming back to you as a boomerang as soon as it hits the other person.

Remember, nothing that happens to you is the other one's fault. So keep trying as many times as you can until you accomplish it, because your environment's change is your responsibility. Remember, you change and the world will change with you. At least, that will be your perception and that is the only thing that matters to you. As all the rules, this also has its opposite side; there are people not interested in changing, for some reason of karma they stay in darkness, but these people you will also learn to recognize; and there are not too many in our world when we are changing. They appear now and then to put obstacles in the way of your evolution. Be resolved without violence, expose your veracity, and don't let them take your peace and conviction. We can make a better world with a collective change.

Believe me, that person will evolve sooner or later towards a healthier consciousness; nobody stays in the shade. We were created to live in the Light. We are Divine seed and will return to the Divine; sooner or later each of us decide how long it will it take.

The "habit" does make the monk

"The robe does not make the monk," is a proverb I've heard since I was a little girl. It was used to illustrate (in some cases), that not everybody who wears a priestly robe is necessarily a good shepherd, but is also used as an expression pertaining to human attitudes and behaviors; for example, not everything that seems to be something, is for real.

This habit which this proverb or phrase talks about is the one defined by the Merriam Webster dictionary as:

"Middle English, from Older French, from Latin *habitus* condition character, from *habere* to have, hold more than give.

archaic – clothing

A habit: a costume characteristic of a calling, rank, or function: *a nun's habit*

Enlarging on the word *habit*-- which in this case is: "a special way to proceed or conduct oneself, acquired for the repetition of equal or similar acts, or originated by instinctive tendencies"-- I can assure you, that the robe (habit) makes the monk.

Eugenio Maria de Hostos said and I quote: "Reflection and experience are telling me, that the habit is to the soul what movement is to the body. That is why I insist in accomplishing the habit of examining myself every day."

Nothing is more certain. I acquired this habit many years ago. No matter how tired I may be, this is part of my nightly prayers and affirmations.

Every night I review what I did and said that day, and I work hard, so as not to repeat what I should not say or do. The words and the acts cannot be undone, but your own soul and your neighbor will appreciate you not repeating them.

That same habit can be used to do repetitions of what you want to change in your life. The first attempts were very difficult for me. I used to leave my house with the sincere purpose of being a person full of light, and my light bulb turned off just at the moment somebody said something to me that I did not like. Then I would get angry and ask myself what had happened to me, because I also felt remorse for my response to the people who attacked me - or at least I thought they did.

All of that is being reformed. It is day to day work, and the habit has helped very much. For example, instead of wishing to be an angel with a halo, the very next day, I'd choose a characteristic of my personality which I wanted to change, and every night I made it a habit, to review it to see how much I had improved in that respect. And I never tried to make a new change in my personality until I was totally sure I had overcome the one I was working on.

In fact, I am still changing; every day there are

new challenges to overcome. Like I said before, this is a job that will last for the rest of our lives. The closer we get to the light, or the greater our effort to attain it, the challenge which we face will be bigger. The good news is that most of the time, you can defeat it in a minute, and the achievement is for life.

THE NEIGHBOR'S SUFFERING

ONCE SOMEBODY SAID IN front of me that nobody knows his neighbor's suffering, and that many of the crimes committed are not because of anger, but because of pain. I did not dare to intervene in the conversation because it involved two strangers talking, while waiting like me, to pay for something at the cash register in a supermarket. I would have loved to be able to talk to that person; she seemed desperate and discouraged.

I would like to have known what kind of anguish made her speak that way, not because of a morbid curiosity – you already know something about my nature; gossip is not my thing. I just think that both of us could have learned, one from another, and that we could have motivated each other. I could have given her a little of what I have learned and she would have explained to me what I had just heard, but had never thought about.

If I think about it now it's because I am sure it is true; but I never stopped to meditate on it. Then, I decided to investigate some human attitudes, and found that even though the outcome is the same, to hurt others, and to hurt oneself have different motivations. I discovered that many murders have been committed without anger, by people full of pain. They are motivated either by the suffering caused to them by the people whose life they have taken, or because of the pain of seeing them suffer, they have taken their lives away, so they will no longer suffer.

Certainly, in day-to-day life it's not always anger that makes a human being attack a neighbor. And although it may seem illogical, a strong sense of justice can turn somebody into an aggressor, even if it is only verbally just to defend a cause or a person.

We human beings are -a conglomerate of ideas, rage, protests, attitudes, weeping, laughter, violence, criticism, rebellions, motivations, etc. All that human beings can be conceived to be is what we are. We are going to get back each and all of those characteristics that identify us to a greater or lesser degree, but all of us – whether we believe it—possess. And we are going to give them a certain importance in our lives – neutralizing each of them, and taking them to a level of equilibrium where they can be used in a constructive manner. Even though the names of some of them may sound to you like something negative, everything in its right measure is necessary to maintain equilibrium.

I understood this when I read in the book of Genesis "Of every tree of the garden thou mayest freely eat: But out of the tree of the knowledge of good and evil thou shalt not eat of, for in the day that thou eatest thereof thou shalt die." Of course, good and evil are two extremes of the same energy. Everything is available to us just by our being and receiving. But we wanted more – as children of The Source we also wanted to be givers; so we decided to get that total knowledge, and now we are being given the permission to be ourselves with all of the characteristics mentioned above, and the ones left in the inkwell, in equilibrium.

What about the death which is mentioned? It is a term used to define the end of one way of living to move on to another. After exercising the power of free will, it made it possible to attain this freedom we posses today. We asked for it, so we are going to use it in the best way possible, for our sake and for all the creation. This is why it's now our turn to evolve, until we become that which we were in the beginning, with this difference. We will have already learned how to be givers, not only receivers. Death as we conceive it, does not exist; it is just a transition from one state to another. It is like you telling the water turning into ice, that it is dying. "Nothing is lost, everything is transformed." Energy does not die and that's what we are.

"*Lips of wisdom remain shut,*
except for the ear capable of understanding.
Wherever the teacher may be, there, the ears of him
who is quick to
receive his teachings, are wide open.
When the ear is able hear, then the lips that are to
fill them with wisdom, will come."
The Kibalion.

CHAPTER XII

✳

WHERE AM I?

A FRIEND OF MINE lost seventy pounds through diet and exercise. She is happy; she loves it. She tells me that when she looks in the mirror she asks herself, "Hello pretty lady, where are you?" Although the weight lost was gradual, she was working on it for a year – defeating temptation. She had bought some pants, too small for her, with the intention of wearing them and looking nice.

She did not care whether it would be fashionable when she was that size, she just wanted to put them on. Temptations would come, one after the other, to make her break her diet and exercise routine, but she went to her closet and looked at her pants, looked at the girl on the label, and promised herself that very soon they would fit her better than they fitted the model.

"I hardly recognize myself, I love myself; I've kept my weight for two years and I am more optimist, happier and I feel I am better with others," she said to me. "The change is so great that when I see my figure in the mirror I ask her for me, because it looks like another person."

The same thing can be done with the spiritual change – to start shaping the previous consciousness little by little, removing those wrong thoughts that hurt us. We are going to start noticing wonderful changes in our personality and, yes, we look physically prettier. That light on your face when you smile spontaneously and happily makes you look radiant. You notice it, and others do, too.

In remodeling your new personality you can, if you wish, include a healthy diet, which brings about physical changes, as the soul is changing. You can do yoga or some other dynamic exercise, if you are able.

Study something related to what you are trying to do, or join a reading club where they discuss metaphysical matters. This way you will have a better understanding and it will be easier for you to answer somebody who asks about your new personality. You will always find them trying to minimize what you do; so the more knowledge you have about what you are practicing, the more secure you will feel. Remember that nobody has the total truth, so do not try to impose. That is called fanaticism and we do not want to get into that.

You will also have your limits. When you're up against a wall, when they ask you something you don't know, simply smile and tell the truth. Say that you're an eternal student of the eternal, and that we only get to know eternity completely when we go back to it; but, if you learned something along the way, you will be happy to answer later on.

Don't feel bad; whoever asks you something knows less than you. Always remember that while making your changes all kinds of challenges will come your way. It's time to overcome, to remember what you are doing and why.

Of course everything has its opposing side, and you will also notice you begin to attract different people – people who have a mentality similar to what you are trying to have. It's time to learn from them and to find a group of friends with the same interests. This makes change easier and your life more beautiful.

Once you think you have made a little progress, look at your soul's mirror and ask, "Hello pretty lady, where are you?" I guarantee it's going to be hard to find yourself because you will not want to go back to your old personality with its failures, weeping, problems, undesirable comments, etc.

However, it's now your turn to reach out to people who were part of your previous world. You must begin to try to do your part in the formation of new people, not under pressure or preaching, but with the help of your unconditional love and your new personality, replete with beautiful examples.

I AM HERE FOR YOU

I AM GOING TO give you examples of affirmations and negations that you will be able to use in the beginning. However, the ideal is that you learn to formulate your own, so you do not use the ones I'm giving you as a pattern, learning them off by heart and repeating them just like a parrot. We want to know – just as when we speak to someone – what we are talking about, with all the details.

I want you to be conscious of what you say each time you formulate an affirmation, because even if it's true that although you say it in a liturgical manner, it is always going to work. I have noticed that when I affirm or deny something with all my senses alert, it gets manifested in a faster way, and that is what we want.

So I invite you to do it in the same manner, fully conscious but above all, being positive that what you are affirming is a reality, and you are completely sure of that. At the beginning you may lack some of the words for what you want to express, but the idea is in your mind and it is working the same. It is going to work – there's no one thing to make it fail if you are totally convinced in what you do.

Once, somebody asked me why some things are manifested first – then others. Remember what I said at the beginning; everything has been given to you. If something has not manifested it's because you refused it, by your behavior or lack of faith; but it is there for you and for nobody else.

When you begin to accept this truth, the things that were meant to happen next in your life will manifest first. When this happens your faith will be stronger, and the others will come in good measure, as the Teacher said, "Seek ye first the kingdom of God and its justice, and all the rest will be given to you for good measure." There's no mistake; that's the way it is. It is not a fairy tale or something similar; it is a truth you can demonstrate to yourself. As I said before, you don't even have to believe me. Just practice it and be amazed at the results.

The good thing about these teachings is that you are not obligated to anything, nor are you threatened with a severe punishment; nobody will burn or refuse you. However, if you follow them you will get to see changes so important in your life, that the certainty of being right will never be able to be questioned. The more changes you make, the more challenges you will have, but more beautiful things will come your way. Of course, if you draw close to The Light, this will light you. The seed which does not produce good fruit is not good seed. You must be very aware of the results of the things you do. If these are good, rest assured that you are on the right path; if you have a negative consequence, look again at what you are doing to find out what you are doing wrong and correct it. All of us fail everyday and much more than you can imagine. When this failure happens we must stop to see who we are hurting with what we did or said. If we have the opportunity to excuse ourselves, let's do it, but watch out. That can't be a diplomatic excuse just because of good manners or for getting away with something for the time being or because we think we had to do it. If that is the case, nothing is happening inside of you, and the opposed energies will keep vibrating between you and the person. If, at that moment, it seems impossible that your excuse can be full of love because you are holding back some anger for what happened or made you act. At night, when everything is calm inside your heart, forgive that person with love and forgive yourself for failing in your process. But also realize in your soul that the person you offended is your same energy living in another body. The following exercises I give you are easy to follow, but I am aware that, like everything else in life, you need the conviction of being willing to do it. You need to make an effort and time to do it; you need not to be tired to do them. You need to tell yourself – it is here and now when I want to begin. I tell you this because the usual excuses for us as human beings are "I am not convinced," "I don't feel like it," or "I am tired." It happens with all the changes which are good for us and that affect our daily routine. Don't feel bad; defeat them.

The desire to change does not make any change in your life; you need to reorganize your mind into a new structure totally opposed to the one you had. If you fail, you are not doing it right; try again because I guarantee you that what I am offering to you will give you the power of using your superior I. Therefore, it will not fail. God does not, and it is your part which you inherited from God which is the one you are going to use.

So go and have fun emptying spaces full of useless things in your mind, organizing it with new things which will truly make sense in your life.

If you empty your house and renovate it, and then

you fill it with new furniture and different decor, how would you feel? That is what I want you to do with your mind. You will feel that same sensation of well-being that produces a positive change.

Do you want that? Well, do it.

Then, you could say as I say to your brother, "I am here for you, I can give you what I've been given." I promise you will never feel a greater satisfaction in your life than this.

CHAPTER XIII

✵

STOP CRAWLING

WHEN YOUR LIFE BEGINS, everything happens in stages. Your first years are very dependent and despite your effort to begin being yourself, somehow your parents sabotage your effort in trying to protect you.

There are parents who want their babies to stay sitting because they consider their back is not ready yet. I see the effort the baby makes to sit down because he or she feels they can already do it, and this is how our race towards our identity and for the right to do what we really want, starts.

It is a natural instinct that makes us wish to discover everything by ourselves, but the greater our effort, the greater the opposition we find in our parents. Be careful the baby does not fall. Don't sit him down because you will hurt his back; the baby is crawling too much and he or she is going to hurt their knees.

The baby already walks but keep him/her in the baby's area to protect him from older kids.

These are only some of the recommendations I hear everyday in the center where I work, but there are some parents completely respectful of what their kids can do. There are others who are afraid of seeing them grow up. In the same manner, going through stages is how you are going to start your new life.

It's very possible that if you are not one who reads an entire book once you sit down, you have begun to practice what you are reading here, so it is very likely you have started to experiment with your first favorable changes and that you like what is happening around you. This can turn into anxiety if you don't get equilibrium because when you are trying to do something and begin to make it real, but your goals are very high, you can hurry up to realize more achievements. It does not work that way.

I've told you how we start in the first years of our existence as an illustration in order for you to compare it with your mental and spiritual growth. It must be in the same manner, just like a baby crawls for several weeks before standing upright and taking his first steps, likewise, our mental and spiritual growth will begin. Each and all of our desires are stages of growth which we have to go through and this is good because you must be prepared for your growth.

I'm going to give you an example and I want you to see it as such. I'm not saying you wish to be a millionaire, what you get depends on you only. I can't predict it for you, but just think that one of your goals is to be a millionaire.

Believe me, if you think that in this very moment you need a change in your life, and you are in a negative stage or you lack great faith, it is very possible that if that money comes, it will go as fast as it came. If not, read the published stories about instant millionaires through the lottery; many of them have lost their fortunes.

Your achievements are infinite, but in order for them to be long lasting and not just a fashion as I have heard many people say, that meditation is fashionable, metaphysics is fashionable, and that Kabala is fashionable, but this is not so. All are disciplines which must be developed little by little, with full consciousness and for all your life. Fashions are discarded, but not our consciousness. At this point in this book, if you have been exercising and restructuring as you read, you can already say you have stopped crawling spiritually, so you are ready to walk, but remember the first steps are shaky. Don't hurry, don't run, you are just taking the first steps.

Remember you are going to walk for the rest of your life; you'll never be a fetus again, you'll never be born nor will you ever crawl again as long as you are firmly walking your way through this reincarnation.

LOOK HOW WELL I WALK

NOW YOU ARE GOING to show off as a baby who starts to walk. The first days you are going to watch to see if people notice your new face, your new attitude and your brand new will to walk erect, from the spiritual point of view. You will concentrate on this affirmation, "Look how well I walk."

Those are your first spiritual steps in public, when you already feel capable with others in this state of transformation. Some will say you look different; others will remain quiet, but believe me everybody will notice it.

As time goes by it will be more noticeable. People who have not seen you for a long time will see you so different they will even say you look younger; especially if you have freed yourself from a painful situation, or if you have let go of a dependency. That new light on your face can't be ignored by anyone.

Even you will notice you look better-- you are not just attractive to others, but for yourself. Many who are reading this might have hated themselves. That new relationship with yourself will increase your sense of security, and the more secure you feel, the greater your ability for achievements. There's no doubt about it.

It is very possible that if you are overweight, you'll begin to loose some pounds because some of you will change your eating habits, willingly. You are not going to want anything that identifies you with your old personality. You will change your activities. Many will start choosing songs, movies or programs without the negative connotations of weeping and suffering and their lives will start flowing smoothly. It's not that the things which bothered them are going to disappear the next day, but their burdens will be lighter and little by little they will go away.

The change will include as many aspects of your life as you wish-- the less attachments you have, the greater your ability to evolve- because each time you break a bond, or a desire to hurt somebody with your actions or words, you are automatically making contact with the light.

This will be explained better in one of the readings I recommend at the end of this book. Okay, we already know we can make changes. We've been experimenting with some unknown things and some others we have lost start coming back into our lives. It all starts to be easier; and when we stumble and fall we get up, shake ourselves, and keep walking. What do we have to do now?

We're going to experiment with the beautiful feeling, to visit one of those mansions which was spoken of by The Teacher: "In My Father's house are many mansions"-- our upper room, our spiritual person, our Superior I, our I am; our personality closest to God; our bodies. How can we reach such a high honor? Through meditation.

MY METHOD FOR MEDITATION

IN REALITY THERE'S NO one unique method to meditate. If we were to investigate, there may be several. The truth is, I do not use any of the ones I learned in the books; I just did that at the beginning. Little by little you experiment and learn from other methods, until you realize you can make that contact in a more personal and comfortable manner.

The written guides are to teach you to begin your way, then you can walk without help from anybody, and you can do it faster than you did with the method you learned.

I'm going to teach you the way I do it, in case you want to use it and then change to your own, or just in case it's more comfortable. And if you wish to do it forever, that is your own decision. What I propose here is that everybody use it. There is no restriction at all, at least not from me.

MEDITATION

YOU CAN USE SOFT instrumental music--a CD or some other source of music, suitable for meditation (I recommend it); or you can choose a quiet place and do it without music. You can also opt for a natural sound, like water from a fountain or one of those devices which record sounds from nature.

They are very good for relaxing.

The important thing is that you can get the last one, to relax. Many people need a little more time because they are nervous and are constantly worried about the difficult situations they are going through. If you are one of them, do not get discouraged. I promise you can also do it.

If you like incense or use aromatic candles, you can use them as long as you don't let their aroma distract you from your concentration, because of allergies or other circumstances. I usually meditate around five in the morning. I like to do all of my exercises when I begin my day; this helps me weather the difficult moments when they come.

I only meditate at night when there has been a circumstance during the day which has pulled me out of my inner peace, and it is threatening to give me a sleepless night. I never let my mind keep me awake and certainly not because of external circumstances. I never use incense or any kind of external help. I did at the beginning; it helped me a lot. This is why I mention it in this book.

That peace during the time when I am alone is incomparable and I can't substitute it with anything else. After learning this, I've never done it in any other way, unless I join a meditation group where this is the rule.

Besides, this formula has helped me to escape when there is an unpleasant situation around me; where my participation is not required, or when I am in public or in a group and the energy becomes so dense that it bothers me.

An escape of even ten seconds creates a regenerating stream of incredible energy, and others do notice it, unless they know you very well and know you are evading. So, we are going to take the first steps for a personal meditation. Afterwards, you will decide whether to revise it..

1. Close your eyes and inhale through your nasal cavities, slow and deep as you can, and retain the air as long as possible.

2. Exhale slowly through your mouth until you feel you have let out all the air.

3. Inhale again, the same as the first time.

4. Exhale again slowly, as in step two.

5. Inhale again and repeat steps one and three, which are exactly the same.

6. Let the air out, following steps two and four-- which are the same.

7. Now you are going to repeat the six steps above, but this time feeling how the air fills your umbilical area, about an inch below your naval. Feel how it totally fills with air.

8. Exhale the air slowly.

9. Again, fill your umbilical area with air to its

maximum, breathing slowly.

10. Exhale again, slowly.

11. For the third time repeat breathing, deep and slowly filling your abdomen.

12. And exhale again until you feel empty.

In this moment you are in a light relaxation stage. You are entering into your inner room. Little by little start loosening your muscles, relax your feet and legs until you feel them light; loosen and relax the arms until they become light. At this moment all your breathing must be slightly paused and relaxed; Loosen your shoulders and let your mind be calmed; in these moments nothing can be more important than the connection you are experimenting with-- The Highest.

You can use this condition to visualize the things you want to get; to create a peaceful situation where there is no discord. You can also send blessings of light, love, health and forgiveness to who might need it.

At this point you are in The Presence. There is nothing you can not get under your Divine contact status; It is not your human mind but your divine mind that is fabricating now.

Take advantage of the opportunity to put your day in order. Visualize and attract that which you are missing at this moment, out of the things which belong to you as the divine inheritance.

When you finish your "trip" to the high spheres of your consciousness, come back little by little. Start feeling your hands, feet, body, and open your eyes slowly.

Stay calm for a while until you come back to the world you live in, and get ready for a better day, full of prosperity.

AFFIRMATIONS AND NEGATIONS

AFFIRMATIONS AND NEGATIONS ALSO have a very great importance in our lives-- especially when we are trying to create a new, happy and prosperous life. Without realizing it, we spend the day decreeing negative things for ourselves: "I am always late." "I have such a bad memory." "I do not smile because my teeth are ugly." "I am so fat I look like a balloon." "What bad luck, everything happens to me." "Anybody sneezing, standing at my side, makes me sick," and many other things we sometimes say, jokingly, about ourselves.

We must realize our mind is not autonomous and it records what we are saying exactly, in a programming mode, and therefore, these are the things our mind creates and recreates constantly about our lives.

When I work with people I realize the amount of negative statements they are making day by day. My ex co-workers didn't know that every time they said something I didn't want for my life, I negated it, saying to myself: "Cancelled."

Because at times, you find yourself so involved in the conversation, that you give your opinion unintentionally, or in reaction to what is being said, although you do not agree. Whenever you find out you are decreeing something negative upon yourself, cancel it immediately. This applies to negative thoughts which assault us because of previous programming, either from our parents, or those learned and recorded in the course of our existence.

AFFIRMATION
(To neutralize fear)

EVERYTHING AROUND ME IS part of the Divine Gift I brought with me in my journey from the Womb of God Father-Mother.

The universe and its elements do not include fear because there is no threat; love is the energy flowing around me.

I am a particle of the universe and I can live with the assurance that only Divine Love moves my actions and the acts around me.

Fear is an appearance and as such, it disappears the moment I negate it.

Father, I thank thee that thou hast heard me.

Affirmation
(To neutralize conflicts)

EVERYTHING THAT IS HAPPENING is not part of my world. I don't even share the idea of a conflict in my mind. I come from a heavenly home which is completely in harmony and conflicts are human creations. By the power that has been conferred on me, I affirm that in both my environment and in my life, everything is harmonious, and that this appearance of conflict exists only if I give it power. All that presents as discord is definitely cancelled in my life.

Father, I thank thee that thou hast heard me.

AFFIRMATION
(To eliminate sadness)

THERE IS NO REASON to let this sadness appear within; my world contains all I need to be happy. This is a human circumstance which has nothing to do with my divine origin. I am grateful for all the things I possess and I rejoice in that, every day. Love fills my life and sadness does not exist.

Thank you God Father-Mother for all that I possess; no matter how small it may look, it is something that serves me within it's capacity.

AFFIRMATION

(To eliminate the appearance of lack)

LOOKING AT WHAT IS within the range of my sight only, the universe is a vast space and it contains all my worldly needs.

I do not have to worry about shortage; it is a human condition created by people without knowledge of the truth, which I copied some time in my life, and it was recorded in my mind.

I reject shortage; it does not exist. I bless the abundance of all that is necessary in my life. Thank you God Father-Mother; for every time my hands open, they are full of all, for me and for my neighbor.

AFFIRMATION

(To eliminate the appearance of illness)

I CLOSE MY EYES and I visualize my spiritual body, full of light, full of splendor, healthy, capable. I see no shadow darkening the perfect health of my energetic body. Thus, this health is part of my human light during my sojourn on planet Earth, enacting my evolutionary process. This perfect health blesses my life and each organ and cell of my body is healthy, now.

Father, I thank thee that thou hast heard me.

CHAPTER XIV

✵

HEALING YOUR INNER CHILD

ALMOST ALL OF US have some unresolved problem from childhood. It is pretty rare that this has not happened. Even those children who have been loved and respected at home can carry around some complex, dormant in their subconscious, caused by some circumstance beyond the control of their parents.

This can be some teacher who did not love them, their friend's parents who made some hurtful or mocking comment, or people in charge of looking after them. Or that seed- which will appear in adulthood could have been planted at home, causing disasters such as lack of self-esteem, uncontrolled ego, social and professional failures, etc.

These things must happen so our destiny, tikkun

or karma can be accomplished. If all our past lives were perfect, and this one as well, where could we find what we must learn to evolve?

We would not be here anymore, but in the Home of The Light, accomplishing our duty as enlightened beings. The truth is, that as long as the circle of our life lasts, we must continue coming back until we learn everything.

Besides the remembrances our genetic memory brings from other incarnations, we have the experiences from our present life, and these began in our mother's womb. Each sensation our mother experiences- whether they are good or bad- will be recorded in our unconscious forever. The same thing happens with the experiences we have after we've been born. Absolutely all that occurs around us is recorded and assimilated by our brain as a record of something, which is a reality of our existence.

When there is a situation in our lives that is related to what we have on record, this programming will be manifested right away or almost immediately.

For example, if you say to a child that he's a fool and that everything he or she does is wrong, in their first job interview or perhaps during a test at school, this will be manifested. It will be very hard for him to do well, although it may be something very easy.

Likewise, if your son or daughter-regardless of how little he sees his or her father beating his mother or vice-versa, the message he gets from that will affect his or her response in a tense situation. And they are very likely to respond with violence.

If a teacher always makes it look like a child's work seems bad, no matter the child's effort, he or she never sees a reward for his or her ability, whether great or little; he or she is creating an adult insecure about his or herself, with a great deal of his or her self-esteem in ruins.

This is why we should care for our children, because as I said before, it is easier to correct them than having to deal with the adult, later on.

I wanted to make this clear because many people do not want to admit that there was something in their childhood which scarred them, and it is important to remember all these things in order to heal them before trying to make a drastic change in our lives. I know a very loving person with a great capacity to be happy, with big doses of love for children, who has told me she had a happy childhood.

She did all she wanted under the supervision and acceptance of her parents; she used to talk in amazement about her mother until one day a situation made her remember that not everything was wonderful. She said it was difficult for her to forgive her mother's infidelity against her father; later, she recalled that her mother slapped her during her fifteen year old birthday party in front of her friends.

What happens is that she wants to be happy and I applaud that; she has managed to put those circumstances out of her conscious mind. She only talks about the positive in her home, but she must work with the negative circumstances, because they are there, recorded, and since they came up that day, I imagine it has happened some other times and will continue to happen.

I am not justifying adultery, but her mother is the only one who knows what pushed her to do that and what lack she had in her life that she didn't know how to resolve in another way. She sees her father just as a father, but not as a man.

Now we are going to take a tour of our childhood to find out the possible obstacles, or the little blocks that were placed in our way, without our parents realizing it.

A TOUR OF OUR LIFE

FIRST, WE'LL BEGIN REMEMBERING the things that are easier; of course these are the ones we had after the age of five or six years old. I am lucky to keep memories alive since I was eighteen months old; this is not common, but I am sure I am not the only one.

When we learn to work with our memory, this will reach more and more into the past. If you try to do it, you could get to your mother's womb and to the point of conception. I have not yet achieved it, but I know people who have done it and they have gained great advances in their evolution, being able to break the patterns acquired before their birth, through their parents' behavior.

You need the same environment you use to meditate; you must be careful not to force the situation because your mind will block it in the same way your computer does, when you try to open several programs at the same time. Remember, your mind is also a computer; it is not autonomous, it gets programmed with data of daily events, for centuries, and if we don't change the programming, we'll continue receiving those documents every time you click on the right word to open them up.

If your parents told you, when you were a child, not to get wet in the rain because you could catch a cold, you can be sure this is going to happen when you get wet. If people who spend their lives following a diet would stop saying they are fat constantly, they would not have to be on a diet. They could just affirm that they are healthy and slim, and that they have a lean body; their brain will do the work for them. Immediately it will instruct the body to stay slim.

Going back to regressive meditation, the easier way for me to do it is going back day-to-day to the past beginning with the most recent day, so that I start training the memory in the exercise of recalling.

If you are uncomfortable or you still doubt you can do it, discontinue it. Don't do it until you trust your capability.

It is not magic or something out of the ordinary; it is your experience, your memories; they are some place inside of you and you can have access to them whenever you like. Moreover, you must exercise the right to do it if your emotional stability or some other things important to you are at stake.

Remember, perhaps the cause of what hurts you today, of the obstacle you have on your way, or the constant access to negative people into your life, can be in your memory. Find it; face it; understand that it was recorded by other people, maybe since your early infancy, but it is not going to rule over your adult life and discard it.

We are going to start by recalling what happened yesterday; it may seem foolish, but most people I asked did not remember all they had done during the day before. Others had to use their agenda and only remembered what they had written; a small group was able to do it, but with a big effort and only after a period of time.

As it happens, we do things automatically, and although our subconscious records them, we do not keep them in the memory. To all this, add the amount of observations, affirmations and negations we hear from our co-workers, and from people around us all day long in and out of our job.

Our brain gets saturated and sends the biggest portion of all this to the hard drive; it stays there until we decide to read it, or an actual circumstance activates it.

So, we are going to make an effort and try to remember, step by step, what we did since we opened our eyes in the morning until we closed them again to go to sleep.

It is very likely we don't remember everything in our first exercises; we could have a personal memories agenda to help us in the first days or months. It depends on the time each one takes; each person has a different pattern.

We could have a little book where we write each thing we do since we have woken up: pray, exercise, wash our teeth, shower, breakfast, I mean, everything.

You are going to start practicing three types of breathing, you'll inhale air through the nose, deeply, the biggest amount of air you can; you will retain it as long as possible without disturbance; you will exhale through your mouth, slowly. You will do this exercise three times until you feel a total relaxation.

When you enter a calm state, there, in your upper room, in contact with your Superior I, you are going to give yourself an order, clear and concise, but do not disturb your inner peace. You will ask your memory to give you a record of all you did the day before since you got up.

Keep in mind, you must not make any effort to

remember because you block yourself. Once you have your picture from the beginning of your day, the other things will flow freely, unless you allow your mind to entertain you with something that may be interesting or bothering you.

If this happens, you must begin the procedure doing the breathing exercises, because your memory has sent you a message that disturbed your peace a little. Mind is always bombarding us with things, which are previously recorded, for a long or short time.

One must learn how to control it, because the mind can become dangerous. In reality, we do not have memory of our past reincarnations and we can receive disastrous orders from our subconscious. I wanted to explain this to you so you don't think you can't do it. You can, this is only a little obstacle which you will know how to remove from your path.

We will give the order again to look inside our memories, and we'll start right when we get up. We are going to do a mental review of everything we did, in strict order until we get to the bedtime.

You are ready to begin your way back to the present. As soon as you feel firm about the present, you're going to try to remember all you lived yesterday. Write it down; if after some time you remember things you did that day and you could not find it in your memory, add it to your notes and write down the date and time when you recalled it.

Everything must have its date and time, so as you advance you realize the time it takes you to remember everything, absolutely everything.

This exercise, from the day before, you are going to do for a month, on average, unless you are completely sure you have mastered the technique from the day before. When this happens, you will immediately start to find out what you did two days before.

And thus, successively; as more days go by with more training, you will have to search in your memories, not into those your mind wants to send to you, but into the ones you are looking for.

You can get a lot of experience in traveling through your life and could also fix many things in your personality which are hurting you, or are stumbling blocks, and you do not know how they came into your life.

It is very important you write down what you are remembering; you must know this will give you clues to get to the hint or hints you are looking for. When you face a memory that is painful or, somehow, has made an impact on your life, you must stop, go back and write it down.

Later, you will begin to investigate in which area or areas of your actual life this is having some repercussion. Then you will have to affirm that this is a circumstance out of your life. It does not matter how many times you have to do it, or how long. The truth is some day it will disappear, it is up to you if is sooner or later.

For example, if you experienced violence at home, you could understand why you attract violent people into your life. Affirming that this is not what you want for you and eliminating it from your life is the only way you can be healed; you must understand that this was the circumstance of another person, not yours.

There are people who jump from one relationship to another during their whole life, and they find the same, or a similar pattern. They do not know why this repeats again and again, and what is worse, they realize something is wrong right from the beginning, but they'd rather keep going because they don't like loneliness.

This happens to men and women, but the majority are females who tolerate it, because of cultural patterns. This is because they have many children, they can't raise them by themselves or because they feel they can't survive without their husband's salary.

Some of them decide to make the change, but they fall again into a similar relationship. With the exercises I offer you in this book you can free yourself from repeated patterns; you can erase a programming and dare to be you. When this happens, look around you; you will see that people who hurt you start to go away and people who are more spiritual and evolved come into your life, with a more positive programming.

Remember these steps are not given to you to remember and blame those who, in one way or another, created in your mind frustrating circumstances. This is a human and natural event; we, as humans, love to find guilty ones – that is why I warn you.

This is for you to heal, spoil yourself and let you know the inner child, once and for all. Your inner child is a superior being, unique, with great qualities – he or she must use for his or her own service and for the Creation's.

A compromise to help yourself is good; blaming others delays the process, because it is the crutch we use to destroy ourselves with no remorse. The biggest cowardice for a human being is hurting oneself, while blaming others for such actions.

So, use that privilege you have. You are able to heal

the inner child using the regressive memory and you can integrate your inner child into your actual life – strong, happy and able to accomplish all of the dreams which were saved in a file of unpleasant memories.

When you achieve this, you'll see it is easier than what you thought to get out of that environmental mediocrity in which you are. You will get to know yourself in such a way that nobody could ever tell you what you have to do, because you are going to know why and what you have been created for and what your calling is in this reincarnation.

Do not let them manipulate you. I have already warned you before that there are people who do not understand what you are learning. It is normal, the evolutionary process is not the same for everybody; their time will come, but do not get behind because it may happen that if those people awaken suddenly to their truth they will not wait for you. This is an individual work, full of conviction otherwise it does not work – you must be sure of who you are.

Reincarnation is something many people still do not accept totally; they have experiences and memories of something they are sure has not happened in this reincarnation, but yet, they fear the idea or do not accept it because of religious reasons.

Imagine if the whole world finally accepts God as not a sadistic being who punishes for eternity. Many religious institutions will see their whole thing about hell falling apart.

That "punishment," if you wish to call it that, is because of your programmed mind to give you security, because you feel it is forgiveness, cleansing of guilty. What you pay here is really called consequence- karma, effect, tikkun, reaction.

It is simply the answer to the universal law of rhythm which is already written and can not be conformed to what you did, thought, said, or manifested even in a written manner. All is mind, everything originates in your mind, everything you manifest had to live there first. So this mental energy is what brings you the consequences, no matter how you executed it.

I hope I have made clear to you the motive of the circumstances that you do not understand in your life; try not to repeat the same mistakes, learn from them that you are not guilty of anything. There are no guilty ones; they are only a consequence of insecure steps we took and when we fell down. As the universal children we are, we have to get up, shake ourselves off and keep going without judging others or ourselves, and forgiving -this is a key point, it does not fail. Love and forgiveness are the basics for a life full of prosperity that includes all that you want.

I cannot ask you not to go wrong because I do it myself, but rather, to learn from your mistakes, that you get them out of your system and that you be happy.

And remember what I said a few pages before, love is the only thing that multiplies when you share it; do not forget it.

I have guided you up to this point. I have tried, with this book, to present the explanation about the steps to follow as simply as possible.

Later we will study in detail, many of the things I mention here, and others I briefly touch upon, such as reincarnation, the beginning of our world through the Big Bang, the law of cause and effect, and others.

In reality, the motive of this book is not the teaching of Metaphysics or the Kabala. These are only mentioned briefly, but I use their principles to help you take your first steps in the realization of your dreams.

Also for you to practice and demonstrate to yourself that you can exercise a way to get out of any circumstance. I showed you some of my accomplishments; it is up to you to believe it. It does not matter; what really matters is what you can accomplish for yourself.

Do you want to start? It is your turn. I hope to hear from you sometime. My address is at the end of this book; I would like to hear not only about your improvements, but also about your achievements when helping your neighbor. You may feel the wonderful need to narrate the biography of your soul to them.

This book has been written with love and it is open to constructive critique and to wise discussion, because correction comes out of constructive criticism, and light comes out of wise discussion.

It is the least I expect from you. This book emerges from the experience of many ups and downs; tears and laughter; just and apparently unjust situations and from the experience given to me by the feeling of the failure in many aspects, but also, from the success of a having had a miracle.

Thanks,

Militza.

Recommended Books

1-Letters to Me
   Alex Rovira Celma
2-The Power of Kabala
   Yehuda Berg
3-Metaphysics 4 in 1
   Connie Mendez
4-Conversations with God 1 & 2
   Neale Donald Walsh
5-Wheels of a Soul
   Rav P. S. Berg
6- The Kabala
   Alexandre Zafran
7-Zohar, The Book of Splendor
   Leon Moises
8-Be Ye Transformed
   Elizabeth Sand Turner (Unity)

Famous quotations to ponder a little.

REVENGE

♦ I speak not of revenge or forgiveness, forgetting is the only revenge and the only forgiveness.

> - Jorge Luis Borges

♦ In taking revenge, a man is merely even with his enemy; but in passing beyond it, superior.

> - Sir Francis bacon

♦ The best revenge is to be unlike him who caused the injury.

> - Marco Aurelio

♦ To revenge a stronger one is madness, an equal dangerous, and an inferior low.

> - Pietro Metastasio

♦ Revenge is the most delicious feast spiced in hell.

> - Walter Scott

♦ Whoever revenges after victory is not worthy of winning.

> - Voltaire

BITTERNESS

♦ Frequently, a man's bitterness is just a child's petrified fear.

    - Franz Kafka

INFERIORITY

♦ No one can make you feel inferior without your consent.

    - Eleanor Roosevelt

HAPPINESS

♦ Human felicity is produced not so much by great pieces of good fortune that seldom happen as by little advantages that occur every day.

    - Benjamín Franklin

♦ Some day somewhere, inevitably, you will find yourself. And that, only that, will be the happiest or the most bitter of your hours.

    - Pablo Neruda

♦ Happiness is not doing what one wants but to loving what one does.

    - Leon Tolstoi

♦ Happiness in life is always having something to do, someone to love and something to look forward to.

    - Thomas Chalmers

♦ Happiness is inward, and not outward; and so, it does not depend on what we have, but on who we are.

- Henry Van Dyke

♦ Many persons lose small joys while they wait for great happiness.

- Pearl S. Buck

♦ We look for happiness like a drunk looks for a handle. We know there is one, but we don't know where it is.

- Voltaire

TRUTH

♦ Who holds truth in his heart must never be afraid of lacking the power of persuasion.

- John Ruskin

♦ It is better to find out the truth by oneself that to have to find it from someone else.

- Aldous Huxley

♦ Truth is totally interior. We don't need to look for it outside of us or want to realize it by fighting with violence against our enemies.

- Mahatma Gandhi

♦ Believe those who are seeking the truth. Doubt those who find it.

- Andre Gide

If at some time, you desire to share your experience, or some doubt fills your heart, you can write to me. According to my time and priority of arrival, I will answer all your letters. I will try to give a little of my knowledge to your hearts.

Remember that nobody has the total truth. Someday we will all unite our pieces of truth and we will have the greater truth. Meanwhile, let's continue working in our lives, on our souls and never stop the journey towards ourselves.

Militza Segura-Landrau
PO Box 268112
Weston, Florida, 33326-8112
USA